July 8, 2018

Richie —

Never stop in
go with love
in your
heart
always

I Made It This Far

Je t'aime

Angelique

I Made It This Far

The First Half of My Life

Angelique E. Constance

BALBOA
PRESS
A DIVISION OF HAY HOUSE

Copyright © 2013 Angelique E. Constance.

All rights reserved. No part of this book may be used or reproduced by any means, graphic, electronic, or mechanical, including photocopying, recording, taping or by any information storage retrieval system without the written permission of the publisher except in the case of brief quotations embodied in critical articles and reviews.

Balboa Press books may be ordered through booksellers or by contacting:

Balboa Press
A Division of Hay House
1663 Liberty Drive
Bloomington, IN 47403
www.balboapress.com
1-(877) 407-4847

Because of the dynamic nature of the Internet, any web addresses or links contained in this book may have changed since publication and may no longer be valid. The views expressed in this work are solely those of the author and do not necessarily reflect the views of the publisher, and the publisher hereby disclaims any responsibility for them.

The author of this book does not dispense medical advice or prescribe the use of any technique as a form of treatment for physical, emotional, or medical problems without the advice of a physician, either directly or indirectly. The intent of the author is only to offer information of a general nature to help you in your quest for emotional and spiritual well-being. In the event you use any of the information in this book for yourself, which is your constitutional right, the author and the publisher assume no responsibility for your actions.

Any people depicted in stock imagery provided by Thinkstock are models, and such images are being used for illustrative purposes only.
Certain stock imagery © Thinkstock.

ISBN: 978-1-4525-7200-0 (sc)
ISBN: 978-1-4525-7202-4 (hc)
ISBN: 978-1-4525-7201-7 (e)

Library of Congress Control Number: 2013906416

Printed in the United States of America.

Balboa Press rev. date: 05/07/2013

Table of Contents

Acknowledgments vii
Introduction ix

Chapter 1   The Pink Candies 1
Chapter 2   Raped at Eight Years Old 5
Chapter 3   Junior High and High School Years 9
Chapter 4   Fitness Saved My Life 16
Chapter 5   The Start of Mental, Physical, and Verbal Abuse 27
Chapter 6   The Divorce from Hell? 37
Chapter 7   Second Chance 46
Chapter 8   Peace 52
Chapter 9   Love 55
Chapter 10   My Healing Process 58
Chapter 11   Reconnecting with the Other Half of My Soul 64
Chapter 12   My Second Step to Healing My Whole Soul 67
Chapter 13   Letting Go of My Family in a Spiritual Way 71
Chapter 14   Another Way to Heal: Visual Body-Scanning........... 75
Chapter 15   Healing from My Second Pregnancy 79
Chapter 16   Fifty-Plus Years to Make a Difference 83
Chapter 17   Sedona: Let the Healing Begin 90
Chapter 18   Sedona: Understanding the Past Life 99
Chapter 19   The Next Fifty Years of My Life 117

Acknowledgments

WRITING THIS BOOK HAS BEEN a huge healing mission for me. I couldn't have done it without the support of my wonderful father, Herve, and my four daughters, May, Marie, Rose, and Isabella. Thank you for loving me and empowering me to share my story with others who need to take charge of their own lives.

I want to thank my friends for their moral support in helping me heal and encouraging me to keep writing. I want to thank my editor for guiding me in my writing and encouraging me to keep going. He told me that my story would encourage women and men to stand up for their own lives.

Last, but not least, I thank my husband, Anthony, for giving me my space while I wrote my story. There were moments when I had to let go and endure crying sessions as I rehashed my past.

I am blessed and grateful, and I thank you all for believing in me.

Angelique E. Constance

Introduction

THIS IS MY LIFE.

My angels have been speaking to me for the past week, asking me to work on my life story. They kept saying, *Write it. Handwrite it. No computer.* I had been using the computer to journal, but I felt that I was not getting the true feeling or story of my childhood, teen, and adult life. I know that once I finish writing this book, I will eventually have to type it, but right now I have to write it by hand. I find that when I handwrite my experiences, the words come from my heart and soul. That depth transfers to my writing, and I can remember everything that has happened in my life.

I was born on May 21, 1962, in a small town in Northern Alberta in Canada. My parents are French Canadian. My father was born and raised in this town. His father was from Quebec, and so was his mother. My mother was born in New Brunswick. She came to Northern Alberta to teach in the early sixties, and it's where she met my father. They were married in 1961, and I was born in 1962. My brothers were born in 1963, 1965, and 1967, and then my sister was born in 1970. We were all raised on the family farm not far from town. We were raised Roman Catholic and spoke French in our home until I started school. After that, Franglais was spoken in our home. What is Franglais? It's a half-and-half mixture of French and English spoken in one sentence.

As a child, I played outside, had my own bed to sleep in, went to church, fought regularly with my siblings, and experienced my mom hitting me a lot. At the time, I thought the hitting was normal. Looking back now, I know that it was very dysfunctional and abusive.

My father smacked me once on my hand because my brother and I were playing with matches. I felt that it was okay for my father to punish me for what I had done. But that was the first and last time he ever punished me.

On the other hand, as far as punishment went, my mother was a whole different story. She hit me every day, even when I had done nothing to deserve it. After a while, I just stopped feeling love for my mother because of the lack of respect she had toward me. I look at my childhood pictures, and in many of them I was not smiling. In the majority of them I was crying. Whenever my mother was having one of her moments, she would hit me—with either a wooden spoon or a leather belt. Eventually she stopped using wooden spoons on me because they would break, so she used the leather belt instead.

The only time my mother didn't hit me was when her own mother spent the winter with us. She didn't dare hit me in front of her mother. At those times, I felt safe. I always enjoyed having my Me-mere stay with us for six months when she came from the east coast to visit. But once my grandmother left and returned to her home, my mother began hitting me again.

As a child—and even today as an adult—I have asked myself, "What have I ever done to you to get hit every day?" My mother still has her moments, but today her way of getting at me is to criticize how I raise my daughters, how I look, or how it's a sin to have such a beautiful life as mine.

How do I handle it? Well, on some days I say, "Whatever, Maman," or I just bless her and let her go. It is her issue, and she needs to work on herself and realize that she is responsible for herself. But in this lifetime, she is so angry and destructive that I don't think she really cares whom she hurts or uses. This is just how it is.

Now her life revolves around how much money she can get from my father in their divorce settlement, because she is on a mission and has turned all of us against each other. Right now, I am only concerned about my father's health. Never in his wildest dreams did he imagine that he would be going through a divorce after being married for forty-eight years. I can see that my mother is mentally and verbally abusive to my father—a disrespect she will pay for later in life. I don't think we are ever going to be close as a family. My mother has been very destructive with her children and is now the same with her grandchildren.

The angels have been speaking to me for a very long time to write a book and share my life stories in order to help others move forward and empower themselves in this world. I have a lot to share with you, and as you are reading this book, some of you may say to yourself, *Wow. What a strong woman she has become!* Some of my stories may shock or rattle you, but then again, maybe some of you will relate and feel that you are not alone.

This universe is a great place to live. Only you can make it the best place possible for you. I am learning and healing every day in my current life. I know there is much more to learn, to experience, and to rejoice in—with what God and the angels have given us. This book was written as a means for me to heal and for others to learn from my experience. My intentions are not to discredit anyone, but I need to heal and let go. I need to move on. In the process, I hope to help some of you let go of your hurts.

No one should experience abuse, rape, or disrespect. We have been chosen to live on this earth, albeit for a short period of time, and we need to learn and understand our life lessons daily. I truly believe that when we die we come back to learn how we could have been better people, or to resolve issues that we could not deal with in our past lives. We all have a purpose, and sometimes we need to come back to better it or to be better people. We are all spirits, and we choose the life we want to experience. We all want to better ourselves. I wish for world peace and lots of love, respect, and happiness for all women and children—and men as well.

Chapter One

The Pink Candies

I WAS RAISED ON A farm, and our first home was quite far from the road. As a little girl, I felt that the farm was my world, and I did not see beyond that.

I remember sitting in front of the TV and watching *The Friendly Giant*. Afterward, my brother and I would play hide-and-seek. In our kitchen we had one cupboard. It was one of those cupboards that stood by itself and had a few doors and a few drawers to store our cutlery. I remember climbing the cupboard, opening the door, and finding a small bottle of pink candies. I took it, jumped off the cupboard, and ran to hide behind the couch. Then I tried to open the bottle to eat those pink candies. I finally got the bottle open and ate all the pink candies, after which I hid the bottle under the couch. I did not think anything about it; I just went off to play with my brother. The day went on, and when it came to suppertime, I ate. But I felt very tired, so I went to bed.

Later that night, I guess my mother found the empty bottle and woke me up. All I remember is that she tried to get me to throw up, but I couldn't, and I fell asleep again. Please remember that I was a child, so I really didn't understand why my parents were upset with me. I woke up in the hospital the next morning, tired and in a bed that had white bars all around. A Catholic nun was looking at me. I didn't see my mother or father around, so I went back to sleep.

A few days later, my dad told me that the "pink candies" I had eaten were actually children's aspirin, and they hadn't been able to wake me up fully. They'd had to rush me to the hospital to have my stomach pumped. My father asked me why I had eaten the pink pills, and I told him I had eaten them because Mom was mad at me. I told my father that I had wanted those pink candies and had been determined to eat them all. My father explained to me that the pink pills were only used when someone was sick. He explained that eating all those pink pills could have made me really sick—or could possibly have killed me. I could have ended up in the hospital with all those machines attached to my little body. The doctors had pumped my stomach as a precaution, because my mother had found the baby aspirin bottle empty.

There is another event that I recall from my childhood. It was in the fall, and I was in my father's black, two-door Dodge car. My mother was driving us to see our father at our second farm across the river. My brother and I usually had to sit in the backseat, but somehow that day I had convinced my mother to let me sit in the front seat beside her. I remember looking out the passenger-side window and thinking to myself how easy it would be to open the car door while my mother was driving. I could jump out and see what would happen to me. At that point in my life, I wasn't scared of death. I just wanted to get away from my mother so she would stop hitting me.

At that moment, I grabbed the door handle and pushed the door wide open while my mother was driving. She started screaming at me and told me to close the door or else she was going to punish me. I looked at her and said, "Bye, Maman," and jumped out of the car.

I grabbed the passenger-side window, which was still up, and held on. I remember looking down, watching the road pass underneath my feet as I was dangling. I was thinking, *If I let go, I can be free from my mother. She won't be able to hit me anymore.* I thought I would just fall on the grass, tumble a little bit, get up and brush myself off, and start running away from her. Then I would be free of her and make a life of my own.

While I was hanging on to the window, my mother slowly stopped the car, pushed herself across the front seat, and asked me to come back in. I looked at her while I was still holding on to the window. The door was still wide open, and I said to her, "As long as you promise me you won't hit me or spank me." I looked her squarely in the eye, waiting for her answer, as there was no way I was going back into my father's car until she answered. I knew what she had done to me before, so I waited for her to speak.

Finally, she agreed that she would not touch me or spank me. At that moment, I let go of the side window, landed on my feet, walked to the back of the car, and got into the backseat. My brother was crying, and I moved to sit behind my mother so she couldn't touch me. She started the car, and we drove to meet my father at the second farm.

When we arrived, she opened her door and pushed the driver's seat forward so my brother and I could get out. We ran toward our father, who was waiting for our arrival. That day, my mother kept her distance from me while I went to play in the field with my brother.

At suppertime, my father took me for a walk and asked me what had happened. I told him I wanted to run away because I was tired of my mother always spanking me for no reason. I told him that if I scared her enough, maybe, just maybe, she would stop hitting me. My father looked at me with sadness in his eyes and told me he would speak to my mother. He would tell her to leave me alone.

After that, my mother kept her distance for a long while, but by winter, the spanking, hitting, and verbal abuse started again. That season, the farming industry was not doing very well, so my father had to find a winter job to be able to pay the bills. Our mother was not working as a teacher at that time, and she decided to stay home for the winter. I remember her telling me that it was now time for her to spank me for what I had done to her in the fall on that day when I'd jumped from the car and hung on for dear life. That was a very long, cold winter for all of us. I remember our Christmas being very quiet, and we did not get many Christmas presents from Santa.

Now that I am writing about these two childhood experiences from an adult viewpoint, I realize that my actions were a way of getting back at my mother. I had been at a point in my life where I had stopped feeling. A child who is being hit pretty much every day becomes sad and feels that no one loves her or is there to protect her.

When my father said I could have died if they hadn't pumped my stomach, my little mind thought, *I wish I did die so that Mother would stop hitting me.* After the pill incident, my mother didn't hit me for a period of time, but unfortunately it did not last. I was around four or five years old when all this happened to me. I remember my parents putting locks on the cupboard so I could not open the doors, but I still did not feel any love from my mother, even after I came home from the hospital. As a child, I was lonely and just wanted to be loved and heard, but I did not get that. I felt sad and wondered what I had done to my mother to make her hit me all the time. She never reassured me that she did, in fact, love me.

I am a mother of four daughters, and we always communicate our love to each other. In every conversation I have with my daughters, over the phone or face-to-face, we say, "I love you." We long ago agreed that if anything were to happen to any one of us during our day or week, our last memory would be of our love for each other. We would not feel guilty because we had not conveyed our love to each other. It would give us peace of mind, because we all would remember the love. How many of us wish we could'a' or would'a' said *I love you* to that special person in our lives—dad, mom, sister, brother, sister-in-law, father-in-law, or other relative—before he or she passed away? My daughters and I agree that saying these words gives us the peace of mind that we are loved. When was the last time you told someone you loved him or her and truly meant it? What are you waiting for? Call that person and say, "I love you." Wait to see or hear that person's reaction. You will be amazed by it. It will make that person's day!

Chapter Two

Raped at Eight Years Old

THIS WAS WHEN MY LIFE as a young, innocent, virgin child changed. I remember it like it was yesterday.

My little sister Gracie was being baptized that Sunday afternoon. She had been born in August, and children were usually baptized a few weeks after birth. It was a cloudy, warm day, and everyone was at the house—my aunties, uncles, and cousins. I was wearing my favorite fake-leather, pullover, brown dress over a crisp, white blouse, and my Sunday shoes.

As my mother was dressing my sister in a white christening gown for her special day, one of my older cousins, Mitch, kept bugging me to come outside with him. Now, understand that this cousin had been bugging me for weeks to come with him because he had something to show me in our farmyard. I kept saying no to him, because I could not understand why he wanted to show me something in our farmyard. I lived there and knew that there was really nothing new in the yard, because my father would have told me if there was.

That day, Mitch asked me again and grabbed my hand to show me what he wanted. As we were walking toward the back of the house, I asked him, "What do you want to show me?"

He answered, "Just follow." He grabbed my hand with quite a firm grip.

Finally, I got upset and pulled myself away from him, said that this did not feel right, and started to walk away. As I was walking toward the house, Mitch ran to me and grabbed my arm and said, "You'd better come with me, because no one is going to believe you when I am done with you."

I was scared, and the look he gave me was very frightening, so I gave up and followed him. We arrived at one of the grain bins in the yard, and he looked around to see if anyone was watching from the distance. Then he pushed me onto the ground and said, "Don't move." I fell to the ground and saw how angry he was toward me, and I was scared. I prayed that someone would come and save me and take Mitch aside and explain to him that his intentions were not acceptable, but no one did.

He raped me repeatedly, to the point where I felt nothing. I asked him to stop, but I was not heard. I remember looking to the sky and asking God to protect me and love me unconditionally. It felt like an eternity before Mitch finally got up and told me not to move until I could not see him in the distance. I realized as I was lying on the ground, numb and speechless, that my life had been changed forever. At that moment, I put all my faith and love in God's hands. As I look back through time at that moment with forgiveness for the people who hurt me, I see that I was healed and became the strong young woman I always knew was in me.

At that time, I looked around for my cousin, and he was nowhere to be seen, so I got up off the ground, dusted myself off, and started to walk toward home. I felt sad, betrayed, dirty, ugly, and empty. I walked very slowly back to the house. When I walked into the house, my mother came up to me to see if I was okay. I looked at my cousin Mitch and then at my mother, and I said, "Yes, I am fine." After that, I went into survival mode. I kept to myself all day, as I felt very sad and lonely.

Thereafter, every time my cousin Mitch visited us, he would rape me repeatedly, whenever he had an opportunity. I was eight years old, and he was thirteen. This went on for a year. After a while, he avoided me completely, and I said to myself, "Finally, he is going to leave me alone."

However, Mitch's family stayed overnight at our house, because they had moved to the big city and needed a place to stay when they came to visit the farm. One night, Mitch's brother Gus started to threaten me. He said that if I told his parents or mine, no one would believe me because I was a bad girl and my mom would spank me. Gus then started to rape me repeatedly. I was nine years old, and this went on until I was sixteen years old.

All of this happened in my parents' home, while my parents were upstairs with his parents. The bedroom door was always locked, and my brothers would knock at the door to see if Gus was there, but he would cover my mouth and tell me to shut up or he would kill me if I made any noise.

Finally, when I was sixteen, I told Gus to piss off (fuck off), as what he was doing to me was very wrong. He looked at me and started to laugh and said that I was a loser. I felt helpless, used, disrespected, dirty, and empty. I recall that in third grade I hit one of my male cousins because I was so emotionally and physically hurt. I would react that way whenever any boys bullied me. I hated boys and men for a very long time. I did not trust any man, my family, or any of my relatives. I did try to reach out to my grandfather, but he could only help me so much.

Looking back today and knowing what I know, I believe that if only one person—anyone—had given me support or listened to me, maybe my life would had been different. I always wondered if my mother knew. As a mother myself, I have taken the time to get to know my daughters, and if I were to notice changes in my daughters' behavior, I would take my daughter aside and ask her what is going on. My daughters know that I will be there for them, as I always have been. They know I love them very much. Children do not lie. They are the most honest, innocent beings. Not getting support or understanding from my parents—and most of all, my mother—was very sad.

As a child, you look to your parents for support and protection, and I was not protected at all by my mother. My father is and was an awesome father, but he was very busy with the farming and working away from home during the winters. My father had no clue what was going on with me. My mother took care of the house, but she also abused me every chance she had.

When you read my story, you can understand that my self-esteem was destroyed and that I was just existing. Every time I reacted or defended myself, I got a beating from my mother. When my father walked into the house after work and heard me crying, my mother told him that I was a bad girl. I was constantly shushed, put down, or spanked by my mother, grandmother, and relatives.

How would you feel? What would your morals be like if you had experienced what I had at a very young age?

Chapter Three

Junior High and High School Years

JUNIOR HIGH WAS QUITE THE experience for me. My cousin Gus was still raping me every time he had a chance until I was sixteen. My years in junior high were not great, as my self-esteem was extremely low and peer pressures were very hard on me. I rebelled a lot in junior high and had no drive to do well in school, so I just barely passed my grades. Girls were mean to me, and so were the boys.

Then I got involved in sports. Volleyball was the sport I chose to do as a way to get away from home, away from my mother's temper and abuse. I enjoyed my classes in physical education, because I felt really good about myself afterward, as I excelled in them. This class gave me the drive to keep living and to look at life in a different way. I hoped that I could do something for myself that no one could take away from me. Sports kept me going in life, and what was going on at home did not really matter. I had a sport that I enjoyed playing, and I was part of a team that did not judge me.

I did not really care about my other classes, as I felt they were very boring, and there was no incentive for me to excel in classes other than my physical education class.

The bullying started in junior high and continued until I graduated from high school. There was one particular girl in my school, whom I had known since first grade, who bullied me until tenth grade. I really could not understand why she treated me that way, as I had never done anything to her. In a small town, there was only one school for the community, and it went from kindergarten to twelfth grade, so the students you started with in first grade would most probably be with you until graduation.

As Annie kept bullying me in school, the other girls caught on and started to bully me as well. They called me names, pushed me around, tripped me, and broke my skipping rope. I felt that I had nowhere to escape from the bullying, because I was abused at home by my mother and bullied at school by these girls.

How did I handle it? Well, the only way that made sense to me was to walk away from the girls whenever they tried to bully me. I was really tired of defending myself, and I just shut down emotionally and ignored them. That was why I got involved with team sports: because Annie was very, very lazy, and I knew that sports were not her thing. I felt safe when I played team sports, as she was not around to bully me with her little group of girls.

By the time I reached high school, I was very much involved in team sports, but of course my controlling, abusive mother always made it difficult for me to attend my after-school volleyball practices. Being a rebellious teenager, I told her that I was only allowed to play one sport a year, and volleyball was the sport I'd chosen, so she couldn't argue with me on that. Thank God, because that was my "out." What I liked about volleyball were the weekly, after-school practices. Being in a small town, we only had enough girls to form one team, and it consisted of seven girls, so I had the opportunity to play all the time. Not once was I benched. That meant that we all had to be in great shape, because we only had one player as a spare. My volleyball coach was the one person who encouraged me to do my best, and I did just that.

I played well, and I felt that I was finally being recognized as both a person and an athlete. My father came and watched me play at my home games, but my mother never supported me in any of my games. To be honest, I really did not want her there anyway.

I thought that being involved with team sports in school would stop the bullying, but unfortunately it didn't. My last year of school was the worst year of my life and the hardest in every aspect—emotionally, physically, and mentally. One afternoon during lunchtime, I was walking out of my class, and a girl named Donna decided to kick me between my legs from behind. I fell to the ground with great pain between my legs and almost passed out. I could not get up from the floor. Donna said that I deserved it.

I looked at her with a confused expression, as I had never done anything hurtful to her. I slowly got to my feet, even with the pain between my legs, and went to the locker room to check on myself, as I felt something running down my legs. I thought that maybe I was bleeding. As I walked to the locker room, I asked myself what had provoked Donna to do such a thing to me. I still question it today.

After I checked myself and realized I was not bleeding from the assault, I returned to class and went on with my day, feeling numb inside. Donna kept her distance for the rest of the year, as she knew that one day I might get her back, but I refused to stoop to her level. If you met her today, you would see that every aspect of her personal life has not been great at all. I firmly believe in karma.

When people hurt you physically, mentally, or emotionally, it turns into a life lesson that can present itself in many ways. It can affect your health, jobs, marriage, and finances. I have seen it work, and I truly believe that God sends us life challenges to learn from. God does not punish, because he loves us, and we need to learn from our mistakes.

That year before our Christmas break, I went through the most hurtful, unforeseen event that ever happened to me, and it caught me by surprise. Two weeks before our Christmas break, two girls from my class did the most disrespectful, unimaginable thing to me. Let me share my story.

One morning during my English class, Mother Nature kicked in. I asked the teacher if I could be excused from the class, and he agreed. I went to the locker room and took out what I needed to take care of my womanly function, and then I returned to class and did not think anything of it.

That afternoon, the Royal Canadian Mounted Police came to our class and told us that money had been stolen from someone in our class and that they would like to question us. The RCMP asked who in our class had left during English, and a few of us raised our hands. I happened to be one of them. He asked if he could question us individually about where we had been during the mishap, and one-by-one we were questioned privately.

When it came to my turn, he asked me where I had gone during class and asked me to show him where I'd gone. I showed him, as I felt I hadn't done anything wrong. As we were walking toward the locker room, I said to myself, *Why would he want to see where I went?* So I took him to the women's locker room and explained to him that I had gone there because Mother Nature had kicked in and I'd had to get a tampon. He asked me where my locker was, and I showed him. He asked me to open it, so I opened it without question. He looked through my locker, saw the tampon box, and pulled it out to look into it.

He looked at me funny and asked me if I shared my locker with anyone else, and I said no. He also asked me if anyone else knew my locker combination, and I said no. He then asked me what I had done next. I looked at him with a concerned, puzzled look before grabbing my tampons from him and walking into the bathroom. That was when he realized why I had been there (duh!), and his face turned red.

I walked out of the bathroom, as I felt that there was really nothing else to talk about. He turned and started looking in the big trash can. He found the empty wallet that had gone missing from the complainant. He asked me if I had ever seen this wallet before, and I said no. He thanked me, and I left to go back to my class.

That evening I received a phone call from the RCMP, and he shared with me that he had been informed by two girls that they had seen me steal the wallet. I was in shock over what he shared with me over the phone. I told him that I'd never stolen any wallet or any money. Why would I do that? I had a part-time job. He told me that he had to follow police procedures and thanked me for my time.

My father asked me what the RCMP had wanted, and I told him about our conversation. My father asked if I'd stolen the money. I said no. I had a part-time job, and I had my own money, so why would I steal? Besides, that was not me, and it would never be me.

The next day came, and as I went into school, the shit hit the fan. Classmates accused me of stealing Julie's money and said, how dare I lie to the cops. Even as they were making this insane accusation, I understood for the first time that it was Julie's wallet that had been stolen, because the RCMP had never told me. I was so upset with these classmates for accusing me of stealing her wallet. I had a part-time job, and I didn't steal—period.

The harassment, the bullying, and the name-calling went on for a week, until one morning I saw that Murdle, a friend of mine that I played volleyball with, was crying. I walked toward her and asked her if she was okay. She looked up at me and said that everything people were saying about me in school was all lies and that they were all framing me. She told me that she was going to put a stop to it and that maybe I should change schools because of what people were planning to do to me. She said she was embarrassed by the school, the RCMP, and the people she was hanging out with. I did not understand all her words at that time, but I was sad for Murdle, as I had always admired and respected her.

After that day, the RCMP called me and said that the charges against me had been dropped. I was surprised that I had even been charged for something I did not do. He asked me to call him if I heard anything more about it, and I agreed. After that, no one bullied me or even talked to me about what had happened. It was like nothing had happened, like it was just one big joke.

I finished my school year, graduated, and went to college. A year later, I was home from college and ran into my cousin Danika, and she asked me how I had been. As we were talking, she proceeded to tell me about her understanding of the stolen wallet.

That morning, Julie had brought three hundred dollars to school in her wallet, because she had planned to go Christmas shopping for her family after school. Danika mentioned to me that Julie had been bragging about the money to Marylynne, another girl in my English class. Well, I guess Marylynne had taken it upon herself to steal the three hundred dollars from Julie's wallet. She then told Julie that she'd taken the money and had no intention of giving it back to her, because she was an out-of-work, single mom.

My cousin proceeded to tell me that the only way Marylynne would give Julie her money back was if Julie called the RCMP to report that her wallet had been stolen. Then they would accuse someone, charge her with theft, and hope that the accused person would pay Julie three hundred dollars to keep everyone happy.

...istened to my cousin, I could not believe what I'd just heard. When she finished telling me what had gone on that year, I asked her why she hadn't told me I was being framed or told the RCMP what was going on. Her reply was that she had wanted to see me go to jail, "just because."

I was so disturbed by her response. I said that cousins don't disrespect each other; they help each other. She looked at me and laughed in my face and walked away. Before she left, she said that I could not report it to the RCMP, because it had been over a year, and after a year I could not charge anyone. I was sick to my stomach because of her behavior toward me. What Danika did not realize was that I'd always had the utmost respect for her. I would never have let that happen to her, as I'd always thought we were close. I guess I was wrong.

That day it came to me why Murdle had reacted the way she had that day at school. Knowing what that group of people had planned to do to me had made her feel terrible, as it had been very wrong to accuse me of something I hadn't done. I always enjoyed my friendship with Murdle, playing on the volleyball team together. She never, ever spoke down to me or disrespected me at all. She was the most beautiful, wonderful person in my life in high school, and I will always cherish our time together. Thank you, Murdle, for believing in me and for standing up for what you felt was the right thing to do. I would have done the same for you as well.

As for Marylynne and Julie, their personal lives have been hurt by divorce and health issues. Whenever people disrespect, accuse, or hurt someone, thinking they can get away with it, they should expect that sometime during their lives their actions will catch up to them in some or all aspects of their lives. And then they are going to be the first to say, *Why me?*

The only way you can resolve your past is to forgive yourself and to ask for forgiveness from the person or persons you intentionally or unintentionally hurt. Only you can heal yourself and make positive changes. If you still feel that other person deserved your mistreatment, then I guess there is really nothing anyone can do for you—other than to listen to you crying wolf and being miserable.

As for myself, I have forgiven Julie and Marylynne and send them love, as they both need to heal in their own time. Life has so much to give back to those who want peace and love in their lives. Respect thy neighbor! Get it?

Chapter Four

Fitness Saved My Life

As a child, I always did some sort of fitness activity, whether it was skipping during recess in grade school, figure skating during the winter season, or riding my bike on the country roads. In my junior high and high school years, it was volleyball during the fall season and track and field during the spring season. It was my escape from home and all the abuse, drama, and lack of respect toward me by my mother.

My big break came after graduating from high school, when I was scouted to play college volleyball. I was really pumped that I wasn't going to be living at the farm and that I was going to college. I would be able to pick a career that would work best for me: working with children in the day-care industry. At first I thought it would be fun and would not involve too much studying, as my passion was to play volleyball.

That year, college was interesting, as I had no life skills at all. My parents were very strict and had never let me go out on weekends with friends from high school. I was scared of the big city of Red Deer and knew no one. I was okay with this, though, because no one could bully me like they had in my home school for all those years. I felt safe, knowing that I wouldn't be judged that way. At times college was quite challenging for me, as I knew I had a lot to learn: how to interact with people and how to apply myself to my homework. But overall I had fun away from my family, and I was making a life for myself.

I Made It This Far

One day after one of my volleyball practices, our coach asked all of us to follow him to the weight room upstairs by the gym area. He showed us how to use the weight equipment, as he felt that we needed to train more to become better volleyball players. He spent ten minutes explaining each position of each machine and how it worked. Some of us stayed, and some of us left. I stayed because I was determined to be the best college volleyball player.

So, there I was in a weight room, with no clue about how to create a daily routine that would work for me. Of course, I decided to be a powerhouse and went to the first machine: the seated leg press. I put on the heaviest weight, sat down, and started to push. At first it was hard, but I was stubborn and determined to make it happen.

As I was pushing each rep, I had no idea that there was a proper way to push the leg press, so I used the full force of my legs. At the top of each rep, I locked my knees because the weights were so heavy. Toward the last rep, I felt a pain in my left knee, but I kept on going because I did not know any better. Once I completed my reps, I got off the machine and continued with the other workout stations, even though my left knee was sore.

For a long time it bothered me, to the point that I couldn't jump high anymore. I was a power hitter on our volleyball team, so it was crucial for me to be able to jump. I was limping so badly that I had to have my coach tape my knee so it wouldn't hurt while I played. It got so bad that when I walked up the stairs I had to go backward, because walking forward put pressure on it. With each step I took, it hurt. After that day, I decided that working out with weights was dangerous and that there was no way I would ever work out with weights again.

Months went by, and my left knee got so bad that I had to see a specialist. After the specialist checked my knee, he booked an appointment for surgery, as it needed to be repaired. He said it would get worse before it got better. That summer I went into the hospital and had surgery on my left knee before I returned for my second year of college. I was unable to play volleyball because of my surgery, and the doctor suggested that it would take some time for my knee to heal become strong again before playing volleyball.

Two months after my surgery, I attempted to play volleyball with the college team. I jumped up to spike the ball over the net, and as I was coming down, I landed on my foot and felt a slight twinge in my repaired knee. I went down to the floor, got up, and said to myself, *I am done.* I walked off the court and retired from college volleyball that day.

That year I did nothing in fitness at all. I just focused on my studies, during which I kept jumping from one career to another, as I was determined to find the career that would be the best fit for me. Well, the end of the year came. I had no diploma, and I was discouraged and had gained thirty pounds.

The summer of 1982, I decided to stay in Red Deer and find work, which I did. I started working during the day with children for the City of Red Deer, but in the evenings I was bored. One day I was walking by a local gym and saw a sign that said they had a special guest coming to town to speak about bodybuilding. I decided I would go, as I had nothing to do that evening.

I walked into this local gym. At that time, it was called Liberty Gym. I don't think it exists today. Anyway, I walked in, and they directed me to the room where this special guest was going to do the presentation. I sat in the chairs that were provided for the event, and suddenly this man walked in. He was my height, six foot two, bold, brash, and fit, with muscles popping out all over his body. He spoke with a deep accent and introduced himself as Arnold Schwarzenegger from Venice, California. He shared with us the reasons why he was involved in bodybuilding and the importance of working out and eating well.

I just sat there, absorbing the information he was sharing with all of us who attended his seminar. Of course, I was a little naive, and my inner voices were saying to me that there was no way I wanted to look like him, with big bulging muscles that were not attractive to me at all. I just wanted to get in shape and lose those thirty pounds I had put on during the year in college.

Arnold Schwarzenegger spoke for two hours on the importance of fitness and why we needed to take care of ourselves, saying that our health and fitness activities would benefit us in the long run as we aged. I decided that I should look into joining the gym, since I was done with college and needed to meet new people and get in shape to burn off those thirty pounds. I went home and called my father to see if he would pay for a six-month membership at the local gym so I could get in shape and stay out of trouble. My father did not like me living on my own in the big city of Red Deer, Alberta, but he agreed to pay for my membership.

The following week, I started to work out at the local gym. In those days, there were no personal trainers I could hire to coach me in working out, so I just watched the other members train and mimicked what they did in their workouts. The owner of the gym came up to me and asked if I needed help. I think he saw that I had no clue what I was doing, so I agreed to meet with him the next day so he could put me through a workout routine.

The next day, I went to the gym after work, and he put me through a simple workout that I could do without always having him help me. As he was training me, he asked me if I'd had any experience working out with weights, and I said I'd had a little. I shared with him the story of my volleyball coach and how he had taken our volleyball team to the weight room and showed us how to use the equipment and then left. I told him I'd injured my left knee and had surgery the summer before and that I was working out to strengthen my knee and to lose the thirty pounds I had gained.

We went through a full body workout that I could do three days a week. It was my first time, and he did not want me to be discouraged or too sore from the weight workout, as I hadn't worked out for a year. Well, after my first session with the gym owner, I was so sore that I wasn't able to sit on the toilet.

Let me describe the full body workout to you. You do chest, back, shoulders, arms, legs, and calves. Training the chest, back, shoulders, and arms was simple, as my upper body was very strong from playing volleyball and doing chores on the farm. But my legs and calves . . . well, that was a different story altogether. After my knee surgery, I hadn't been able to train my legs. The only exercise I did was swimming and riding my bike all over the city, as that was my only transportation.

The next morning, I had to go to work. As I got out of bed, I fell to the floor: my legs were that sore. I got up painfully and pulled myself up by grabbing onto the bed. Once I was sitting on my bed, I said to myself, *Just breathe and take one step at a time.* At first my legs felt like heavy logs. Then, step by step, it got easier, until I went to the bathroom to do number one. When I turned to sit on the toilet, I had to put my hands on both side walls to slowly lower myself. Oh, was that painful. I know, as you are reading this, you can relate.

When I was finished doing number one, I had to get up. Well, I just could not get up, as my legs were not cooperating with me, so I decided to curl myself forward and fall off the toilet. What else was I going to do? I had to get ready for work. So there I was on the floor with very sore legs. I rolled to my right side and pulled myself up with the aid of the bathtub, as it had a railing on it for the shower door. Finally I got up and took a deep breath. I thought to myself, *Is working out truly worth all this pain?* I got myself ready for work.

I was living in a basement suite, and of course there were stairs. I looked up and asked my legs to please work with me. I took another deep breath, and taking one step at a time with the assistance of the walls, I climbed the stairs. I finally made it to the top and walked toward my bike, got on it, and rode to work.

As I was riding my bike to work, I could feel that my legs were getting less painful, unlike what I had experienced while getting ready for work. I made it to work and worked my shift with sore legs. The soreness of my legs took a week to go away, but I still went to the gym, and of course the members teased me, as I looked like Frankenstein when I walked. Maybe you can relate.

I was truly grateful to the owner of the gym for taking time from his schedule to train and coach me in understanding the value of working out with weights. That same year, I moved to Edmonton. There were no jobs for me in Red Deer, so I had to move where there were jobs available, and that was the big, big city of Edmonton, Alberta. I moved in with my aunt and my uncle for about two months. That gave me a chance to get myself organized and to find a job and a home for myself.

The first week I was in Edmonton, I found a job in the retail industry. That same week, my aunt helped me find a place to move into. That fall of 1982, a guy friend from my hometown called and asked me if I wanted to work out with him at his gym. At first I said no, as

I really did not enjoy training with weights after all. Nic kept calling me, pretty much every opportunity he had, and every time we spoke, he encouraged me to come back to the gym. He kept saying that I had great legs, and he reminded me that fitness had always been important to me when we were in high school.

I finally agreed to go to the gym with him—after I eventually clued in that he just wanted to be my friend and had no intention of dating me. I just wanted to get him off my back. As he was driving me to the gym, I thought to myself that women with muscles were not considered attractive. He kept telling me that I had the physique and the drive to be a female bodybuilder. From that day forward, he encouraged me and kept me on track with my workouts—four days a week, with weekends off—and eating clean.

I have been training with weights and going to the gym now for thirty years. I was twenty years old when I started working out with weights, and it was a blessing in disguise, as it helped me stay focused, driven, and determined to be the best in everything I pursued in my life, whether it was career-related, personal, or spiritual.

That same year, my friend was getting ready for a bodybuilding competition, and he invited me to come and watch him with our dear friend Charles. I agreed, as I had grown up with Charles, and it had been a long time since I'd seen him. I had no clue what a bodybuilding competition was, but, hey, it was an evening out with two of my hometown friends.

As I was sitting in the audience watching the event unfold, they announced categories for men and women in various weight classes. Class by class they came out, and finally my friend came out with the other competitors. His group did compulsory poses, and then he did his own posing routine with music that he had chosen.

I found it fascinating the way each competitor would strike a pose, and how defined their bodies were, and how each striation of the muscles was so defined with each pose. I was in awe of the beauty, and I respected their hard work and dieting.

Then the women came on stage, and they did the same thing. At that moment, Charles turned to me and said, "You should be on that stage, because you have what it takes."

I looked at him and asked, "Did *he* put you up to this?"

He started to laugh and said, "Yes, but I see the potential in you, and you can kick those women's butts on that stage." From that moment, I decided I would attempt to do one bodybuilding competition and would see how it went. That night we went out to celebrate my friend's success, and the following morning I called him and asked if he would be interested in helping me get ready for the next bodybuilding competition. He agreed. I had no clue about what I was embarking on, no clue about dieting or about how to get ready for a competition, but with his help, I thought I had nothing to lose.

In the eighties, women who competed or even worked out in a gym weren't really welcome, as the men at the time felt that the gym was for men only and that women should stay home and take care of the house and make babies. I remember that most of the members were men, and maybe a handful of women were interested in working out at the gym. The locker rooms were quite interesting, as the men's changing room was huge, and the women's changing room was, well, the women's bathroom. Because of my stubbornness and determination to train at an all-male gym, I made it work for me. After a while, the men enjoyed having women in the gym, as they felt that it was a nice change of scenery from seeing all males.

I started to train for the upcoming bodybuilding competition. My friend helped me with my diet the best he could, and he briefly taught me how to pose. He coached me on what to expect on stage. I had to prepare a sixty-second posing routine, and I also had to purchase a bikini for the event.

As the weeks came and went, I trained five days a week with weights, ate as clean as I could, and tried to understand how much or how little to eat. I did not weigh anything, as my friend told me how big my food portions had to be and that I was to eat a lot of veggies. My cardio training was on one of those stationary spin bikes with a painful seat, and thirty minutes felt like an eternity.

Eight weeks later, I was at my very first provincial bodybuilding competition. In 1982 there was no weigh-in or competitor meeting the evening before, as it was all done the morning of the event. We were asked to be at the event at 7:00 a.m. to begin our weigh-in. We lined up in our categories, and one by one we were each weighed for our class. I was in women's middleweight, which was 114 to 122 pounds. I weighed in at 121 pounds, so I just made my class. The competition started at 9:00 a.m. with prejudging, so we all went backstage, as the spectators were waiting to come in to watch the event.

I was so scared of not knowing what to do once I was on stage—until a woman named Lynda, who was competing as well, came up to me and asked if this was my first time, and I said yes. She asked me if I knew how to pose, and I said, barely.

She said that once we were on stage, I should just do whatever pose she did, and that was all I had to do. So, off we went onto the stage. We lined up side by side, facing the audience, and the head judge started to call out the poses we needed to do. As he called each pose, I looked at Lynda and mimicked her. I was so nervous that I couldn't wait to get off that stage, as there were only seven of us. Finally, they asked us to leave the stage, and we all filed out to the back of the stage.

I thought I was done, until someone asked if I had my cassette with my posing music. I looked at him fearfully and gave him a tape, and then the judge called my name. I walked onto the stage, and everyone was looking at me. You could have heard a pin drop, as it was stone-cold quiet. The music began, and I started to pose. I totally lost my focus and kept doing the same pose over and over, until I said to myself, *Do something else*. Once I felt I was done, I waved good-bye and ran off the stage.

That was the longest sixty seconds of my life. That evening, we had to return to the competition for the awards. We were called up class by class, and when it came to mine, they called all seven women in the middleweight category and gave us our awards. I placed fourth, which I felt was great for my first competition. I was hooked. Even though I was so nervous, it felt amazing that I had accomplished something I'd never thought I would have done.

I learned so much about myself that day. I had never thought that I would have been able to achieve my lofty goals of working out, eating better, and being accountable to myself. The experience provided me with determination, the will to keep going, no matter what, and the will to live again. At that time, I had felt that I had no value in this life.

Now I was driven and passionate, and bodybuilding gave me hope that I could do anything I truly put my mind to.

Since that fall day of 1982, I have done twenty-five contests in thirty years. I placed third and fourth for many years, but I set new goals after each competition, one at a time. I was determined to get my pro card without the use of steroids, which at that time was a common means that woman and men used to win. I was determined to do it naturally, no matter what other men and women said to me. They said that if I did not do steroids, I would never win at any level.

I had so much fun getting ready for each competition, and I was determined to reach my goal. It really did not cross my mind whether or not I would get my pro card. I thought more about the idea of winning in an honest, natural way. I found that when men or women did steroids, their personalities took a turn for the worst. I had a saying: *if you choose steroids to win, you've sold your soul*. I wasn't going to do steroids—or lose my soul or my inner and outer beauty—for a trophy.

My dream came true in 2001. I won my title at the Canadian Natural Pro Bodybuilder Championships. I was thirty-eight years old and a mother of three daughters at that time. In 2006 I placed third in World with WNBF (World Natural Bodybuilding Federation) in New York City. And finally, before I retired, I placed first in Master Figures, 45+ category, with NPC. I was so pleased with my success and the fact that my fourth daughter, Isabella, was there to watch her mother win for one last time. Her sisters, May, Marie, and Rose, had had the opportunity to watch me win in 2001.

Fitness truly saved my life, because it gave me something to focus on and work toward, setting my personal goals and getting to know who I really was. With everything else that was going on in my life, even as a child, I would go and play outside or ride my bike, just to enjoy the freedom away from the abuse. With weight training, I worked on myself while staying away from my abusive husband at that time. It helped me to become a strong, driven woman and to escape from all the abuse and distractions that I was experiencing in my personal life.

I totally enjoyed watching my body transform into a beautiful sculpture while eating clean, as it made me feel light and grounded with a clearer mind. It kept me focused and taught me to not worry about the what-ifs. I just kept working on my personal goals and made them happen, no matter what. I also learned how to adjust my goals and dreams as I reached my goals in all aspects of life. If something didn't work, I adjusted my plan accordingly, so I could move forward and reach my goals. I find that when I am not training consistently and being accountable to myself regarding my health and wellness, I lose focus, and then I start to doubt myself. I haven't failed at all, but it is so easy *not* to go to the gym and eat clean.

Now that I am retired and not worried about the next competition, I go to the gym three to four days a week. I keep myself accountable, making sure that every meal I eat—which is four to five meals a day—includes protein, veggies, and some good fats and carbs. I try to stay away from sugars, white carbs, and junk food. Because I have dieted and competed, I have gotten to know my body well. I know immediately how my body reacts when eating clean and how it reacts when I eat junk food. When I don't eat clean, the farts come fast and furious—enough to gas yourself. You can probably relate, because I know, as you are reading my book, that you are laughing and wearing a big smile on your face.

My suggestion to you is to start working out with a thirty-minute walk, yoga, weights at home or at the local gym, an hour of workout classes, or spinning classes. You need to find some sort of stress relief for yourself. If you have been through the abuse I have experienced, you cannot keep it inside you, or it will eat away at your soul. Take it step by step. The first step is to start eating clean. You need to take control of your life and be accountable to yourself.

You can do it. Stop feeling empty or sorry for yourself. Stop being a victim, as it does not serve you, and your soul is crying for you to take care of yourself. Fitness truly saved my life. If I hadn't had a way to escape from my inner pain and disappointments, I probably would have fallen deep into depression, done nothing with my life, and closed my soul up to everyone and everything, barely functioning until the day I died.

My goal today is to keep working out and to adjust my training routines to coincide with my fitness level and age, as I am fifty now. I will continue to eat healthy foods, to meditate, to work with healers, and to heal within, as I am the most important person to myself.

Today, please go out for a walk with Mother Nature. Talk to your God, the divine one, your angels and guides, or whatever higher power you believe in, and ask them for help. They are waiting for you to wake up and rejoice as you start to recognize the beautiful person you are. I would love to hear about your positive changes, your personal accountability, and what steps you took to heal within yourself.

I believe in you and adore you.

Chapter Five

The Start of Mental, Physical, and Verbal Abuse

IN 1982 I WAS COMPETING in my first bodybuilding competition, and I placed fourth that year. I was quite pleased with my placing, since it was my first bodybuilding competition.

The next morning, I was invited to Florence's home. At that time we had just started dating and getting to know each other. When I arrived at his home, he asked if I had brought my competition suit with me and wondered if I would go and put it on. He wanted to take pictures of me posing.

I didn't think anything about it, so I went inside his home and changed into my posing suit. We went outside in the backyard, and I started to pose. I was feeling very good about myself for placing so well in my first bodybuilding competition. Florence asked me if I would take pictures of him as well, and I thought nothing of it, as he trained at the same gym. As I was taking pictures of Florence, I noticed through the camera lens that he had a very mysterious look on his face. Suddenly, out of nowhere, he kicked me in the face and knocked me out. When I woke up, he was standing on top of me. He said to me that I deserved it. My jaw hurt from the kick. I got up, went into the house to change, and left.

Now, you would think that I would have ended the relationship at that point, but no, I did not. At first, I hung up the phone when he called me at home. He came to my house and knocked at the door, and

I refused to answer it. He booked appointments at the tanning salon where I worked so he could talk to me, and I asked him to leave.

Today that would be called stalking. Because I was very naive and did not date much in my teen years, I thought it was a normal thing guys did when they were in the wrong. He kept calling me and visiting me at my workplace, until I finally asked him to leave me alone. He did back off for a little while. Then one night he called me at home and apologized to me and asked if we could meet up and talk. I agreed.

Now, please understand that I am a strong individual, but at that time I was very lonely, and I desperately wanted someone in my life. I only saw Florence once a week on Saturday nights, as he had told me that he was busy with work and was unable to take me out during the week. I found it quite interesting that when he did take me out on our Saturday night dates, he would pick me up at 7:00 p.m., and by 10:00 p.m. I was back at my house. At times he would sleep over, but when I woke up in the morning, he would be gone. This went on for two years, until I got to the point in my life where I had to end it, as I felt that our relationship was going nowhere.

Then in 1984 I decided to go back to college and get my career in order, as I felt that the job I was working at was boring and had no future for me. I was a single woman again, and being away from Florence felt like a huge load off my back. Going to college gave me a sense of freedom, but I also felt that it was going to make a difference in my life and finally make a very decent income for me.

One Friday night as I was home doing my homework, the phone rang. (This was one time in my life when I wish we'd had caller ID.) I answered it, and at the other end of the line was Florence. I felt like hanging up the phone, as I had ended the relationship and was finally in a good place in my life. He asked how I was doing, and I was quite blunt with him and asked him what he wanted. He said that he was wondering if I would be interested in going out that night as friends. I thought about it and agreed that I would go out with him—but only as friends. He agreed and told me what time he would pick me up. So, off we went—as friends.

We had a great time together, and I thought nothing about it. We had a few drinks and visited with a few friends of mine. When it was time to leave, we left, as I'd already had a long day from college classes. When we got to my house, he asked if he could come in and chat, and I agreed. I told him that it could only be for a short time, because I was tired and had had a little too much to drink. Well, one thing led to another, and before I knew it, we were in my bed, having sex. Yes, that's right: sex.

The next morning, I woke up and he was gone again. I never heard from him. Three months passed, and then I began to get sick every morning at school. I thought maybe I had a bad case of the flu, so I called my doctor and made an appointment. At my appointment, my female doctor checked me out and did blood work on me. She knew me well and knew that I was very healthy, as I trained at the gym five days a week and ate very clean food. She asked me in a joking way if I would consider doing a pregnancy test. I agreed but laughed. I didn't believe I was pregnant, because I hadn't seen Florence for three months. Off I went to get the pregnancy test done, and then I went home.

Well, that evening I got a phone call from my doctor, and she asked me if I was sitting down. I asked her what was up. To my surprise, she told me that I was pregnant and that I needed to come and see her the next day for an ultrasound to see how far advanced I was. I agreed to do so and set a time with her for the next day.

I was devastated. I called my mom and started to cry. On the other end of the phone, my mother asked me what was wrong, and I told her. Now, remember that my mother had abused me while I'd lived with her at the farm for eighteen years, but I still could not believe what she said to me. Her response to my devastation was: "Well, you play with fire, and you pay," and she hung up the phone. I continued to cry. I had just reconfirmed that my mother had never supported me in anything that happened in my life.

I slept horribly that evening, thinking, *What am I going to do? I am single, I'm going to college for my future, and I have no money to provide for myself, let alone a baby.* I was mad at myself as well, for on the night I'd had sex with Florence, I had asked him to wear protection, and he had refused. He'd said nothing was going to happen. Yeah, right.

I called Florence and told him the news that I was pregnant and that I had an appointment the next morning for an ultrasound. There was a pause at the other end of the line, and I asked him if he had heard me. More silence. He finally came around and said, "You're pregnant?"

I said yes, and I also reminded him of his remark that night three months ago, when we'd had sex and he'd said not to worry. I told him I was going to see my doctor the next day for an ultrasound. I said that she wanted to talk to me about my options about keeping the baby or aborting it. I shared that with Florence, because we were not together. I was considering abortion because I was going to school, and there was no way I was raising a child on my own.

He said he was coming over to my house right then and that we needed to talk about the situation, as he felt that he was responsible as well. He came over, and we talked most of the evening. He talked me out of having an abortion.

The next day I went to my doctor's appointment, and my doctor did an ultrasound on me to see how advanced I was in the pregnancy. To my surprise, I was already three months pregnant. She suggested that, because I was three months pregnant, it would not be wise to have an abortion. I did tell my doctor that Florence had come over the night before and talked me out of abortion and that he would help me with raising the baby.

Life went on, and Florence and I got married two months after I found out I was pregnant. I was still going to school, finishing my studies, and Florence went to work during the day. After school, I would return to our home by bus, but things started to change. Florence didn't come home until really late in the evening.

When Florence came home after a long day at work, I would ask him, "How was your day?" He would tell me it was none of my business. I was shocked by his remark to me. We were just newlyweds, and I was quite taken aback by his rudeness toward me. I would make his supper, and he would turn to me and say, "Is this edible?" Then he would laugh in my face.

Finally one day, after hearing that insult from him, I grabbed his plate of food, threw it in the garbage, told him he could make his own meal, and walked way. He started to scream at me, saying that I was his wife and had *no voice* in this marriage. I said that I *did* have a voice and he'd better back off.

The late evenings continued, until one night his friend Jack came over for a visit. I left the living room for a minute, and when I returned, Jack and Florence were not in the living room anymore. I heard some noise in the kitchen, and as I walked into the kitchen, I could not believe what I saw. They were kissing.

I was disgusted and pointedly asked them what the hell was going on. Both of them looked at me and said nothing. I looked back at both of them and walked out of the kitchen in disgust. Please understand that this happened in 1985, and this was not acceptable at that time. I asked Jack to leave and told Florence that he was gross. Then I went to bed. We never spoke about it after that.

The late nights continued, and the secret was out, but as a Catholic girl with no support from my family, I had no one to turn to about what I had witnessed. I delivered our daughter that August, but Florence's relationship with Jack continued.

One Sunday afternoon, Jack asked me to meet him, as he had something to share with me. I met up with Jack, and he told me that Florence wanted to leave me because he was in love with him. I gave Jack a funny look, as I did not understand what he meant. I asked Jack what would happen to me and my daughter.

Jack said that he had told Florence he needed to be responsible for his family, that he had to stay because it was the right thing to do. I had been so naive about what was happening between Florence and Jack, but I knew that what they were doing behind my back was wrong. I was so empty and confused. I was lost—to the point that I stopped feeling and went into survival mode for my daughter and me. I had no one to turn to or talk to about what was going on.

This went on for two years, until one night Florence came home upset and said that he and Jack were no longer friends and that it was all my fault that their relationship had ended. I was shocked that they had still been seeing each other, as I'd thought they were no longer an item. Man, was I surprised.

A few nights went by, and Florence's brother Andre came over to visit us and to see his niece. We were sitting in the living room, talking, and Andre asked me how things were with us. I stood up and told Andre that I wished his brother would talk to me and stop keeping secrets from me.

Florence leaped out of his chair, grabbed me, threw me on the living room floor, and began to choke me. I tried to fight him off, but he had me pinned down so that I could not use my arms or legs to kick him off of me. I screamed to his brother Andre to get him off of me. Florence was screaming at me at the same time and said that he was going to shut me up permanently. Andre pulled Florence off me just as I had passed out.

A few minutes later, Andre was beside me, trying to wake me up. I finally came to. Florence was in a corner of the living room, shocked by what he had done to me. Andre said he would take Florence away from us if I promised that I would not call the cops on him. They left the house.

After I sat on the couch, asking myself what the heck had just happened to me, I walked to the kitchen and dialed the phone to call the police. The police officer who answered the phone asked how he could help me. I told him what happened, and he asked me, "Where is your husband now?" I told him that Florence's brother had taken him away from our home. The officer asked me if I felt that he would return that night, and I said no. He asked me if I was okay, and I said yes. Then I proceeded to tell him that he had tried to choke me but that his brother had saved my life.

The officer asked me again if I feared that my husband would come back that night to hurt me, and I said that his brother had told me he was taking him away from the house. I told the officer that I felt safe but that I had a baby as well. He said to call 9-1-1 if Florence came back. I agreed.

After I hung up the phone, I walked into my daughter's bedroom and watched her as she slept. It reminded me that, a few days earlier, Florence had said that our daughter had fallen down the stairs while I was at work. I had asked him at that time if he had tried to hurt her, and he had replied that it was her fault. I had looked at him and said, "She is only two years old." I silently promised my daughter that no one would ever hurt her again.

I went to bed that night and wondered what I should do. I was so empty and confused. I had no one to reach out to. A few days later, I received a call from Andre, asking me if he and Florence could come over to the house to talk. I agreed. The doorbell rang, and I answered the door. They both walked in, and I could see that Florence was very sheepish and embarrassed about what he had done to me a few days earlier. I asked Andre to stay, as I did not trust Florence, and I told them that I had called the cops the night he assaulted me. We talked, and Florence apologized for what he had done to me. He promised me that he would never hurt me again.

But he lied. That summer, my cousin from Ottawa came for a visit with her mother. My mother called me and asked me if they could come over to visit for a few days, and I said yes. The next day, my cousin was at my front door with her mother and my mother. I was so happy to see my cousin Terry, as it had been a very long time since we had seen each other. I welcomed them into my home. We visited and caught up on what had been going on in her life and mine. She played with my daughter May. It was just a wonderful day to have her over.

The next morning, Florence was home from work to visit with my relatives and my mother. That morning, Florence was not himself. He was acting in a bizarre way, and I couldn't figure him out. I had to go into my bedroom to get something, and as I was walking toward my cousin in the hallway, Florence decided to kick me between my legs. I fell down to the floor in pain. My cousin Terry started to curse at him and asked him what the heck he was thinking, saying that I had done nothing to him to deserve that abuse. Florence looked at my cousin and said that I deserved it, and then he walked away as if it was not a big deal.

As I lay on the hall floor in pain, my cousin Terry came to me and asked me if she should call the cops. I said yes. Finally I had someone who was going to stand by me. As Terry helped me off the floor, her mother and my mother came into the hallway and asked what was going on. My cousin told them what Florence had done to me. He was back, standing in the hallway as well.

Terry told our mothers that we were going to call the cops and charge him with assault. My mother told my aunt in a bold voice,

"Don't get involved. It's their problem." My cousin and I looked at each other and could not believe what we heard. My own mother just stood there as if nothing had happened. She didn't even ask if I was okay.

Terry was so upset with her mother that she told Florence to leave the house and not return until after they'd left. That afternoon, my cousin, my mother, and my aunt left for the farm, and again I was left alone with no support. The mental and verbal abuse from Florence continued, because he had seen firsthand that I had no support from my mother or aunt. Whenever we were out visiting family, he spoke poorly of me in front of them, and no one said anything against him. If I spoke up to defend myself, I was told that I was making it up and to shut up.

This went on for fourteen years. During those fourteen years, Florence would work very late, sometimes until four o'clock in the morning. When I approached him about it, he replied that he had to work late. I knew deep down in my soul that he was lying. I figured that he was having affairs with both men and women.

Then one day I was out with a friend of mine for a break from the children, as I just needed some girlfriend time. At that point in my life, I had three daughters. When I came home, the girls were home by themselves. I asked them where their dad was, and they replied that he'd gotten mad at them for fighting over something. He had lost his temper with them and had punched the bathroom door, telling them that if they didn't stop their fighting, those dents in the door would be their faces next time.

As the weeks and months went by, Florence's abusive and destructive ways continued. He would kick the bathroom door down if he felt the girls were taking too long to get ready in the morning. He pushed one daughter down the stairs, because he felt that she was going too slowly down the stairs. He punched holes in the walls. All of this happened when I was out visiting or when I was at work. I would come home and see what had happened and ask the girls if they were okay. They said yes, in fear of what Florence would do to them next time I was not at home.

I approached Florence and asked him what was going on with him, and he would say, "They deserve it. It's my message to the girls." Then he would walk out of the house, and I would not see him until the next morning. He would call me from his office to let me know that he was not coming home that night because he had to work late. He would walk into the house at 5:00 a.m. and head back to work by 7:00 a.m. This went on for years. Please, explain to me how anyone can work those hours for fourteen years and still function in a positive, healthy way. I know I couldn't.

Then one night in 1999, I finally decided to take my blinders off. I told Florence that evening that our marriage was done. I feared for our lives, living with him, and I said that his abusive, destructive ways were unacceptable. I also told him that I knew he was having affairs and that they weren't even with women all the time. He stood there and laughed in my face and said to me, "You will never divorce me. I own you."

I looked at him in shock, but I said in a very controlled voice, "The only person in control of my life is myself and God." He laughed in my face, turned away, and walked out of the house.

It was time for me to stand up to him and take charge of my life again. I had always worried what others would say or what my family would think. Well, that night I really did not care what they thought, as I had to take responsibility for myself and my daughters' lives. It was not right for them to go through this type of home environment. It was not safe for any of us to live with an abusive husband and father in our home. I could see that my daughters' grades were going down and that the home environment was not healthy, so I had to do what was best for all of us. I finally recognized his patterns of abuse over the past years—his outbursts and abusive ways. I had to do something before he did something to all of us that could potentially cost us our lives. He had gotten away with it too many times, even when my mother was at the house visiting. I had to get a restraining order to get him out of the house, as he refused to leave. He felt that he was the man of the house and that there was no way he was moving out.

I recall one night when he came up to me as I was making the girls' lunches for the next day at school. He said that maybe I should move out with the girls, as the house was in his name, because the girls and I didn't deserve to live there. As I looked at him, I started to laugh and said that the mortgage was under both of our names. Whatever, jerk.

Finally he left, and we had our home again. My daughters and I felt safe and at peace. We went on with our lives, and I went back to work to make an income for all of us to live on. I'd had to do something, because I was determined that the abuse the two older daughters had experienced from their father was not going to progress to the youngest. Their father had abused them mentally, verbally, and physically while we were living together. It was time to move on to a better life, because my daughters and I deserved it.

What would you have done in a situation like this? Would you have tolerated it and stayed for the sake of a marriage? Or would you have left a toxic relationship the first time someone tried to kill you?

Chapter Six

The Divorce from Hell?

WELL, IT HAS BEEN TWO weeks since I last wrote in my journal. Maybe it's because of the title I gave to this chapter. I think everyone who reads my book will be able to relate, because most of us have probably gone through—or are currently going through—a divorce. It was the most trying time in my life, but it was also the best time of my life.

I filed for divorce from Florence in March 1999, because I'd had enough of his lies, his abuse, and his absence from home every evening. My family did not have a clue how abusive Florence had been to all of us. He had assaulted me many times and had always told me that no one would believe me. He had also hit our first and second daughters, and the youngest daughter was about to be next. I have read many articles about abuse. They say that to end an abusive relationship you need to break the vicious cycle, and that was my intention.

I feared for my life and for my daughters' lives, so I had to take the next step—serving Florence with divorce papers. After that, he had fifteen days to get himself a lawyer. On the sixteenth day, I asked Florence if he had found a lawyer. He looked at me and laughed and said no, that he would never divorce me, because he felt that he owned me.

I looked him square in his eyes and said that only God and I owned me. No one else did. I walked away from him, realizing that he was going to make it very difficult for me because he was losing his scapegoat.

The months went by, and he made our lives a living hell. He came home from work and demanded his meals, because he felt that I was his wife and making his meals was my job. Well, sorry. There was no way I was making his meals, because as far as I was concerned, we were done.

Now, most of you are probably wondering about this situation, because you would assume that he had moved out. Hell, no. He refused to move out, because he felt that it was his house, and there was no way he was moving out. So he moved downstairs into the spare room. He stayed there for a couple of months.

I remember one night I was so tired from my day that I went to bed early. Florence was downstairs watching TV with the girls, until I heard a fight between the two older daughters—something Florence loved to see. They were fighting, but that night it was not the normal sister fighting. I heard the oldest daughter screaming at her father, and then it was silent. I lay in bed, wondering if I should get up and go downstairs to see what the heck was going on—or if I should leave things alone, as their father was with them. I didn't hear anything more, so I went back to sleep.

The next morning, I asked the girls what had happened the night before, and my oldest daughter said that her father had hit her across the face to shut her up. I looked at her face to see if there were any marks, and there wasn't. I hugged my daughter and said to her, I am going to take care of this, and he won't ever touch you again. I went into the kitchen where Florence was making himself breakfast and approached him. I asked him, "What gives you permission to hit your daughter across the face?" He said he could—and always would—hit the girls, because he was the man of the house.

One thing about Florence: he was very moody. I remember one time when I had just returned home from work. He was home with the girls, and I noticed that the bathroom door had been punched in. I asked him what had happened. He said that our daughters had been taking too long in the bathroom, so he'd decided that he would punch and kick the door down. He had then pulled one of our daughters out of the bathroom, because he felt she was taking too long to get ready. He also said that the holes in the door could represent my face and that I'd better behave as well. I told him that if he touched me I would contact the police and charge him, as he had a history of violence after what he had done to me years before.

After six months, I finally had a restraining order served to him at his office. That day, my lawyer suggested that I bring the girls to a friend's house. He felt that Florence might try to go into the house, and he feared for my life and for the girls. I knew about what time he came home, and I made arrangements with a friend to watch the girls that day so I could deal with Florence.

When the girls came home from school, I told them that we were invited out for supper and to get cleaned up from their day at school. Then we left. After supper I told my girlfriend that I needed to step out for an hour, as she had known beforehand why I was leaving. I walked up to the girls as they were watching the television and said that I had to do some quick business and would return to pick them up. I left the house and drove to mine. I knew Florence would be there waiting to get into the house, because I had changed the locks during the day.

When I arrived at my home, there he was, sitting on the front porch, waiting for me. He had a pissed-off look—the look he always had when he was going to hit me. I stayed in my van and called the police. The officer asked me if I felt endangered, and I said yes. Ten minutes went by, and then three cop cars came to the house. Florence saw them come around the corner and took off. He realized then and there that I was not joking anymore and that it was time for him to go. Since the police were there, I got out of my car.

As the officers approached me, they asked if the person who had run away was the one endangering me, and I said yes. They walked me to my home and stayed for about half an hour to make sure that he would not return. They asked me if I was okay, and I said yes. As they were leaving, one of the officers said that if Florence returned to the house I was to call them, and they would take care of him. I locked up my home and went to my girlfriend's house to pick up the girls, as they had school the next day.

As I was driving to pick them up, my mind was going a million miles an hour, wondering if Florence would show up at our home and kill us all while we were sleeping. I had to have faith that God and the angels would protect us and that everything would be fine.

I arrived at my girlfriend's house, picked up the girls, hugged my girlfriend, and thanked her for being there for us. Then we left. On the way home, my daughters asked me if everything was fine, and I said that I was going to protect them, no matter what, and that we could sleep in peace tonight.

My youngest daughter, Rose, said to me, "Daddy is not coming home anymore, right, Maman?" And I said, "Yes, your daddy won't be coming home anymore to abuse us." There was silence in the van, and then we all began to cry from the sense of relief and sadness. We got home and went to bed, as we were all exhausted from our day.

The next day while the girls were at school, I called Catholic Social Services to book an appointment with a counselor so that we could all talk about the divorce and the abuse that the girls and I had been exposed to.

The day of the appointment came. The counselor, who was an older woman, was very soft-spoken and so kind. She spoke to all of us and explained that what their father had done to them was not normal and not right. She also explained the cycle of events that build up to an abusive individual. She said that what he had been doing to their mother and to them was not acceptable. She explained to my daughters the reason why I'd had to get their father out of the house, and that it was the right thing to do because I was protecting them. She asked the girls if they had any questions, and they said no.

As we were leaving, the counselor turned to me and said, "Angelique, you are the rock of the family, and you are going to make it. Just take it one day at a time, and be there for your daughters, no matter what. I hugged her and thanked her for her time. As I was driving home with the girls, I thought back to the conversation and felt that this counselor was the best one I had ever worked with. She was so very sincere, passionate, and caring in her message to the girls and me.

After one year of separation, it was time to get the divorce finalized. To my surprise, I learned that my lawyer, Billy, who was representing me, had discussed with Florence what I had asked for in the settlement—which was not much. I asked Billy if Florence had his own lawyer. Billy said yes, but that Florence was great guy and that I was making the biggest mistake of my life by divorcing him.

I looked at Billy in complete shock. I couldn't believe what was coming out of his mouth. I told him that from now on he must not speak to Florence anymore. Florence was only to communicate to Billy through his own lawyer. I also said that there was no way I was going back to Florence, because I feared for my life and what he would do to the girls.

As the weeks went by, Florence would call me on the same days that I had meetings with Billy and would repeat my conversations with Billy regarding settlement proposals. Florence said in a very vindictive way that he wouldn't divorce me, as his intentions were to break me emotionally, mentally, and financially. He said that I wouldn't have a choice and would have to come back to him, begging to have him back in my life.

I was sick to my stomach and said to myself, *Not in this lifetime am I going to have Florence move back in the house.* I hung up the phone and called my lawyer and told him that I did not appreciate his being in contact with Florence. Billy said, "Fire me, and good luck."

So I called a female lawyer by the name of Betty, who was highly recommended to me. I called her office and spoke to her assistant. Her assistant took my number and said that Betty would contact me by the end of the day. She asked the name of the lawyer I was currently working with. I gave it to her over the phone and thought nothing of it, as I thought that maybe it was protocol among lawyers.

Well, the end of the day came and went. The next day, I got a call from Billy, and he told me that Betty had contacted him. I don't know what he told her, but he said that she wouldn't work with me.

This bullshit went on for two and a half years. All I wanted was a peaceful divorce. Florence was the one who had cheated on me with both men and women, abused all of us at home, and kept us broke financially so that I could not spoil my daughters like I wanted to. I did not want spousal support, because if I did, he would make my life miserable. In his mind, it was his money, and I was lucky to be in his life. Whatever. All I wanted was the house to provide a roof over our heads, and child support for all three daughters. I could go out and get a job to provide for my daughters and myself. Florence had been in the auto body business for sixteen years and was doing very well, but I did not want half of his business. He could afford to purchase a place of his own, and I would be able to afford the mortgage payments and live a peaceful life with my daughters.

But no, that did not happen. I had to sell the house. My lawyer, Billy, was not working toward my best interests, and I was very stressed out. I felt I had no support and nowhere to turn.

Now that I look back, there were many red flags regarding Billy's representation of me through the divorce process. One situation that stands out to me occurred when we had just started working on a settlement to dissolve my marriage with Florence. I was in Billy's office, and he sat back in his chair and started to share with me some generic information about a female client he represented. He told me how he had helped her with her divorce and the settlement she wanted from her husband. He also said he had communicated with her ex-husband about what she wanted as a settlement. Billy told me that he felt she was asking too much and wanted to teach her a lesson.

I should have immediately decided to look for another lawyer, but because of my mind-set at the time, I just dismissed the conversation as information, not a sign of things to come. I was learning of improper communications between the opposing lawyer and the soon-to-be ex-husband. My lawyer boasted about providing the husband with details of what the wife wanted in settlement, as it had the potential to be a seven-figure divorce. Billy said he made sure that the procedure was emotionally and mentally difficult for the wife to make sure that she would end up with nothing.

Billy also told me that his fees had exceeded what he and the wife had agreed on. I asked him what had happened. He said that her settlement was less than she'd wanted and that her ex-husband was happy about what Billy had done for him. I looked at Billy and asked him quite frankly, "Is that your intention with me?"

Billy said no, because the settlement I was looking for was nowhere near the millions involved in the divorce he had described to me. He also said that my fees would be nothing like the fees he had charged that female client, as we were not dividing up a large sum of money or property.

I asked Billy, "Why would you do that to any women?" His response was that she needed to learn her lesson, that she didn't deserve anything. I told Billy that I was very uncomfortable with his business practice and that I should end his services now, as I felt that he might do this to me as well. He looked at me and said that no one would take me as a client, because I didn't have much for a settlement. At that point in my life, I was so emotionally beat up that I really did not know any different. I just wanted to get this divorce done so that my daughters and I could begin a new life.

Looking back now, I should have listened to my gut feelings, as it turned out that he was not looking out for my best interests or that of my daughters. He wasn't even a qualified divorce lawyer, which he told me after everything was over. If, at any time in your life, you run into individuals like Billy, listen to your gut feelings. I should have listened to mine, but after he told me that no one would take me as a client because my settlement was small, I thought maybe he was right. I should have let him go and asked about other options from my friends, other lawyers, or other professional people I knew. I could have inquired about assistance for single mothers who need legal service without big fees. Maybe I could have received a better settlement. As I reflect back on that fiasco, I search deep within myself to find the message I needed to learn, which I have. The message was this: truly listen to your gut feeling, and in the end, you will thank yourself.

At that time, even my girlfriend Lynne was turning away from me. I had felt that the only person who could truly help me through those trying times was my best friend, Lynne. She had been through a bad divorce before meeting her current husband, Marcus. I felt that she would support me and maybe give me hope that there was light at the end of the tunnel.

But other people in her circle of friends put their noses into our friendship and really pulled us apart. I was an emotional basket case. I was not myself at all, and I reacted in ways that were not typical of me. Oh, how I miss my best friend, Lynne, and I hope that someday in my life we reunite and have the friendship we had with each other once upon a time.

The day finally came, and the settlement was done. It was signed, sealed, and delivered. What did I get? Are you wondering? Well, I got full custody of my daughters, monthly child support of eight hundred dollars a month, and twenty-two thousand dollars in settlement.

But the best was yet to come. My lawyer, Billy, took eleven thousand dollars in final fees for his work. What work, really? After more headaches than you can imagine, I was left with ten thousand dollars. I asked him, "Do you recall last month when I asked you for the final invoice total and you said forty-four hundred dollars? Please explain to me where you suddenly came up with a final invoice of eleven thousand dollars.

His answer was that the paperwork and settlement had taken a little longer than they were supposed to. I looked at him with disgust and walked away. As I was walking away, I realized that he'd never had any intention of helping me and my daughters to a better life. So, do *you* feel that I got a good settlement? I feel that I was taken for a ride, taken advantage of by my lawyer and ex-husband.

I also believe that when a person is disrespected, lied to, and abused by a lawyer, the lawyer will be negatively affected somehow in his own life. The consequences may relate to his health, career, or the people he hangs around with. Bad behavior always comes back to bite you in the ass. I know we need to learn life lessons, but I also know that when people take advantage of others' misfortunes to benefit themselves, those same challenges are going to present themselves to the predator in the long run, and he may not know how to deal with them. I always wonder what life lessons have come into Billy's life in these past twelve years. I have a sense that this life has been very challenging and that he is not doing well emotionally, mentally, or physically.

Florence and Billy had only one thing on their minds, and that was to demoralize me. I have forgiven them both for their lack of respect toward me. They are disrespectful cowards and liars. Really, when I think about it, they had nothing better in their lives than to try to destroy me. It could have been an amicable divorce. We could have been friends, which would have been the best situation for the girls. But it wasn't meant to be.

Today, God has blessed me with a wonderful life, and it has made me a stronger woman. I know I can survive in life, and I respect people for who they are. God always gives us life challenges, and my life since the divorce has been fun, interesting, and peaceful.

How would you have handled yourself in a situation like mine? We all need to take care of ourselves, and dissolving an abusive marriage to protect yourself and your family is top priority. It is not about what your family will think about your decision; it is about you and your family having a better life and becoming stronger individuals. My personal goal after the divorce was to heal, move forward, and have open conversations with my daughters. I wanted us to do things together that we could not have done before, to encourage each other to do well in our lives. The bottom line was this: I wanted my daughters to feel safe, loved, and supported.

Just last year in 2009, I finally felt that my daughters knew who was the rock in their lives: me. They know who they can turn to if a situation or challenge comes into their lives, because I am there to guide them and suggest solutions. I am so proud of my daughters, of who they have become as individuals. I can sleep at night, knowing that they are strong, beautiful, and smart women.

Chapter Seven

Second Chance

DURING THE PROCESS OF MY divorce, I met someone who was going through his own divorce as well. We had a lot in common, and it was the perfect time for me to have a male friend in my life that was going through the same things I was. Some people felt that it was to soon for me to get involved with another man. They felt that I should stay single for at least six years.

It's funny that people assumed I would quickly jump into someone's pants just because I was single. Whatever. I really just wanted a friend that I could talk to—especially at times when Florence and my lawyer were very hard on me and it affected my health and my way of thinking. It was just so refreshing to meet someone who was athletic, positive, fun to be with, and nonjudgmental—and who was going through his own divorce, experiencing his own bad days with his ex-wife and divorce proceedings. And he felt the same about me. It was comforting to know that we had someone to reach out to. That was it.

What people did not realize was that I had mostly kept to myself while I was married to Florence. Whatever was happening in the privacy of my home was just that: private. No one knew. People only saw me in a good mood, always positive. I felt seriously alone, being essentially single for fourteen and a half years, married to a man who cheated on me with both men and women, who worked long hours, who was verbally, physically, and mentally abusive. To whom could I have turned? I had seen other people share their concerns about their own lives, and people just judged them or didn't talk to them again, as if they had a disease. So I'd kept my problems to myself all those years—until I filed for divorce. Then people approached me and said they knew about it. I would just smile and walk away from them, because I did not feel that I had to give them an explanation.

Before I got involved in a serious relationship, I wanted to take the time to really get to know the person. I was not in a hurry. I needed time to get my feet wet out there, to see what I had missed out on, as I hadn't been much more than a housewife, and I hadn't worked much at jobs. How could I? Florence had made it hard for me to work full-time with the girls in school. I would get a full-time job, and sometimes I would have to work late. He would phone me at work and say, "I won't be home for the girls, so you'd better leave your job, or I will call social services and tell them that you are an unfit mother." Then he would hang up. So I would go to my bosses and tell them I had to leave, and the next day I would come to work, only to find out that I was fired.

So, for me to get into a serious relationship was out of the question. I needed time to heal and to look out for myself and the opportunities for me as a single mother. It was just nice to have a guy friend—who, by the way, lived out of town, so I had my space. Whenever he was in town for business, he would call me and ask if I could meet up with him for lunch or for a workout at the gym. It was nice, because it was fun, not serious. It was great to have a guy friend again.

Florence and I had arranged that he would get the girls two weekends out of each month. I did not trust him, and I felt that one week on and one week off, would not work, because my daughters would be alone all the time during the week he had them. I needed the girls to feel safe in the solid environment of their own home, without being abused by their father. A weekend twice a month with their father would be short, but it was enough time for the girls to spend with their father.

One Friday evening without the girls, with nothing but peace and quiet at home, I asked the angels and God if it would be a good time for me to get into a relationship, because I felt that maybe it was time for me to start dating.

I pulled a sheet of paper out of my desk, and at the top of the page I wrote, *My Ideal Partner*. Below that title, I started to write down what I wanted in an ideal partner. This is what I wrote. He had to be Roman

Catholic, without children, athletic, fun, respectful, lovable, loyal, and faithful. He had to accept my daughters as individuals. He had to be a successful businessman or in a strong business career—and tall, over six feet, not short like my ex-husband.

I folded the page and asked God and the angels to bring me my soul mate when God felt I was ready for it. Then I released it to the universe. I let go and let God. I closed my eyes, took a deep breath, and tucked the folded piece of paper into a journal inside my desk.

That summer, I was invited to a Special Olympics golfing event. At first I declined, as I felt I would not be much fun to be around because of all that was going on in my personal life. One of my dearest friends, Darren, who was on the organizing committee for the Special Olympics, found out that I had declined the invitation. So he called me and asked why I was not attending the event, and I explained my reasons to him. He said he felt that I would be an asset to the group of celebrities there and that I should attend to give myself a break from all the personal issues I was encountering. So I agreed that I would attend as one of the celebrities to help raise money for the Special Olympics.

The following weekend, I drove to Red Deer, Alberta, to support the Special Olympics event. It felt great to go away for a few days and not worry about anything other than myself. Once I arrived, they had a supper for the celebrities and the guests who had paid a fee to play golf the next day with their celebrities. I sat with my team of golfers and had supper and a pleasant visit with my team.

After supper, everyone left and mingled with other professional athletes. I just sat at my table alone, drinking a glass of white wine and enjoying the time without the hassle of my personal life. As I was sitting there, I recognized one of the celebrities—a professional hockey player. I noticed him and he noticed me. I smiled and looked away.

Before I knew it, he was at my table, asking me why I wasn't mingling with everyone else. I said that I just wanted to stay put and relax, as I'd just had a year of pure mental and emotional turmoil. He looked at me and said, "Me too," and we both started to laugh. He then said, "If you ever need a friend, I am here for you."

I laughed and said, "Thank you for the offer, but no." I would not ask you to feel sorry for me, as it was my decision, and I am very happy with the decision I made for the betterment of my health." He understood and left the table to visit with his teammates. After I finished drinking my glass of wine, I got up and saw my friend Darren. I thanked him for the invitation and said good night.

The next morning, I woke up and got myself ready to go to the golf course to play as a celebrity and raise money for the Special Olympics. As I was driving to the golf club, the morning sun was out and shining brightly. The air was crisp and oh so fresh, so I took a deep breath and thanked God for this wonderful day. When I arrived at the club, everyone was sitting at their tables, chatting it up with their teams and eating breakfast. The event started at 8:00 a.m. sharp, so I finished eating my breakfast, walked to my golf cart, and waited for my team. My team slowly gathered around our golf carts. A horn signaled the start of the tournament, and off we went.

It was an eighteen-hole game, and I thanked God for golf carts. I don't know if I could have walked it. Maybe I would still be there today. To be serious, it was my first time playing, and I found it to be very boring, hitting a tiny white ball with golf clubs that my dad had purchased for me when I was eighteen years old.

My clubs were made of wood. That's right, wood. The guys on my team had a lot of fun with my clubs, because we all know that men need the best of the best when it comes to golf clubs. They asked me if they could have the honor of hitting with my clubs, and I said, "Sure. Have at it." Then we laughed. The day continued, and the holes came and went, until I remembered the letter I had written to God and the angels about the ideal partner for me.

Well, I was on the eighth hole when I remembered the guy who had come to my table the night before as I was drinking my glass of white wine. I heard a voice across the field calling Angelique. I said to myself, "Who in hell is calling my name?" I turned to see where the voice was coming from. And there he was at the eighteenth hole, which was right across from me.

I waved and called hello and started to laugh. As I looked at him, I noticed that he was hard to miss, because he was six feet nine inches tall. I had a sudden sense of confirmation that he was the one. I looked at the sky and said to myself, "Really, God? Right now? It's only been six weeks since I wrote to you about my ideal partner."

I heard a quiet voice saying, "Yes, he's the one. He is the one you need to learn from in this lifetime." I felt a sense of peace within myself, and I waved to Anthony as I drove off with my team in our cart.

After we finished playing eighteen holes—and oh my God, it felt like it took forever to get it done—we returned to the club where they had awards for the ten best teams followed by a supper. My team placed seventh, and we received our prizes. It was cool, as I had used my wood clubs and had never played golf before, so I credit my team for doing a great job.

Once the event was over and everyone was getting ready to leave, Anthony came to me and asked if he could have my phone number. At first I said no. He asked if he could have my pager number, and I said yes, because I thought to myself that it wasn't my home number, and if he did call me, then I had the choice to return his call through my pager. We said our good-byes, and I returned home to my daughters.

Weeks came and went, and Anthony did call me on my pager, but I just didn't feel like contacting him because of what was going on in my personal life. I was a personal trainer, so I had a pager for my clients, as I did not have a cell phone. I did not want my clients to have my home phone number.

One day I got a page from Anthony that said it had been three weeks and he hadn't heard from me. He hoped I was well and said that he understood if I didn't want to speak to him. I felt like a schmuck, so I decided to call him. To my surprise, he answered the phone, and we chatted. He wanted to hire me as his trainer to get him ready for training camp. I agreed that I would train him.

As the weeks came and went, I trained Anthony as he prepared for training camp. We started to hang out more and more—to the point that one night, while I was alone, I pulled out the paper I'd written about "my ideal partner." As I was reading it, I realized that it described Anthony.

I sat back and started to laugh. I called Anthony to share with him what I had done before I'd met him, and I told him about my "ideal partner" list. He started to laugh as well. After that, our relationship grew steadily stronger—and today we are husband and wife.

I have always had faith in God, and I was open to possibilities. I was at peace with myself that God would come through for me. I never questioned when it would happen, because at the time I was going through a horrible divorce and I just did not feel any urgency to meet someone.

When life challenges present themselves, do you ever wonder if your request to God and your angels for help will come soon? Have you ever made a wish list to describe your perfect partner? What are you waiting for? It's quite simple. Take a piece of paper and write "The Ideal Partner" at the top. Then start writing what you would like in an ideal partner or soul mate. Don't over-think it. Let it come to you without effort, and have fun with it. Once you are finished, reread it and put it away someplace where you know you can find it later—after your ideal partner or soul mate presents himself or herself. Now, be patient. Don't go out there like a mad man or woman looking for that person. Let go and let God. Your match is out there. Who knows? You may already have met. He or she may be staring you square in your eyes right at this moment.

I wish you all the best. Have fun.

Chapter Eight

Peace

PEACE WITHIN. PEACE. THE PEACE sign. Peace be with you.

What does *peace* mean to you? Have you ever really felt peace? Have you taken the time to think about what peace means to you?

Here's my feeling about peace.

As a young child, I felt peace within myself. Brought up by my abusive mother, I found ways to escape from the turmoil and disruption of my home life. I would find the tallest tree in our farmyard and climb it. At times I had to work really hard at it, as I was a petite girl. It took everything I had to pull myself up to find a tree branch that I could sit comfortably on. Once I was sitting comfortably, I would look out to the horizon and take a deep breath to inhale the fresh country air and just feel the peace within me. At the age of six, that was the only world I knew: the farm and the town where I went to Sunday Mass and to school during the week. During the summer, we didn't go out much, but when Sunday morning came, well, I celebrated in my heart that I finally got to go to town and be away from the farm—and the house—for a short time.

Every chance I got, I ran away to climb my big tree—my heaven on earth—to escape my abusive mother. I would close my eyes and imagine that someone was caressing my face with gentle, loving hands. My long, black hair danced in the wind, moving across my face and shoulders as I enjoyed the peace of being safe in my own world.

For me, *peace* meant sitting in my tree and listening to the sounds of the wind blowing, birds singing, and cars driving by the farm, spinning rocks off their tires. The trees and leaves talked to each other as the wind shook the branches, and I just lived in the moment. It was the peace and quiet that I truly enjoyed. My mother wasn't screaming at me or telling me what a bad person I was—which I wasn't.

I made believe that the trees were huge arms, hugging me with love and protecting me from everything. It felt like the tree branches were rocking me like their own baby, and I would fall asleep with no fear, just peace and quiet. When I woke up, I felt like my world was the best world ever, as I was at peace with myself. It always gave me hope that when I grew up I would be able to move away from the farm and be free from my mother and have my own peaceful life.

Today, as a grown woman, mother, wife, grandmother, friend, and mentor, I find that wherever I go, it's not quiet. There's construction everywhere. People are always on the go, in a hurry to get to where they need to be. Birds don't even sing as much.

When was the last time you actually took time for yourself and really stopped to listen or to feel peace? For me it has been a very long time—too long, actually. Even when I do take that moment of peace, I rush it. We think we are far too busy to take the time to feel, to breathe and say, "Ahhh." Why do we do that to ourselves? We don't really reflect on that particular day in our lives, the person we have become, or the work we have done to heal ourselves and work toward better lives.

What are we doing to be at peace with ourselves and our surroundings? Have we become so disconnected with ourselves that we have forgotten how to feel the peace within ourselves? Are we afraid that if we feel, we will realize that we haven't taken time to enjoy the peace and quiet in our own lives and there can be no return?

No. Only you can take responsibility for your own peace and the ability to feel again. What or who is stopping you?

As I write this chapter, I feel that I am stopping myself from taking time for myself and feeling peace within me again. So, today and hereafter, I am going to live for the present—right up until the day I take my final breath—and be grateful for every challenge that crosses my path, embracing the life lessons that I need to learn from it. Every day, I wake up and thank the universe for my peaceful sleep. I reflect upon what my day will be like, and I feel grateful for my health, that I am able to go to the gym and work out for the betterment of my body and soul.

When was the last time you lay in bed in the morning after a night's sleep and felt truly grateful for the body God has given you? When was the last time you really felt in touch with yourself, when every inch of your body felt peace and gratefulness? Maybe today is the day. Just lie in your bed and caress yourself in a loving way. Run your hands along your arms, chest, abs, legs, face, eyes, and ears and through your hair. Focus on every body part as you take a deep breath and exhale. Wiggle your toes and fingers. I bet it has been a long time since you really thought of yourself and your body. Today, take the time, and when you are all done with the breathing techniques, lovingly say, "Thank you," and feel the blessing.

Being at peace with yourself and being in tune with your body allows you, every morning, to say "I love you" and feel it, because your body does hear you and feel your spirit of appreciation. Your body, soul, and spirit truly miss you. You need to start feeling grateful for the body you have been blessed with—any shape, size, or height, whether or not you have dimples on certain areas of your body—because you are very special and beautiful, inside and out. The only person who matters and loves you is *you*. Be at peace with that. Once you start to feel your spirit, your body will respond and start to heal itself, because you are at peace with *you*.

Start tomorrow morning, and continue every morning thereafter. Relish those few minutes to be thankful, take a deep breath, and say *good morning* and *I love you*. Say it until you truly feel the peace within you.

I love you. You are perfect.

Have an awesome, peaceful day. Love you.

Chapter Nine

Love

WHAT DOES *LOVE* MEAN TO you and me?

Well, it is 4:36 a.m. on Monday, December 6, and I am tired of my life at this moment. I am tired of crying over my life and all that has transpired during the past years—all forty-eight of them. I know you are asking yourself about the title of this chapter, as I have not yet mentioned anything about it—other than the third word.

Right at this moment, I feel alone. My right ear has been pounding for the last four weeks, and I can hear my heart beat in my right ear. What does it mean? Am I burned-out to the point that the angels are trying to send me a message? Am I trying to do too much with my current studies? Do I feel that it's too much for me? Are those old feelings coming back from the time I was a young child in school and not doing my best because of my mother's abuse at home and the bullies in my class getting away with their abuse because their mothers were teachers at the school? Am I losing my mind, wondering if can I do it all? Can I manage it all—the house, my daughters, my personal life, my marriage, working toward my career and my dream of becoming an inspirational woman, a mentor and motivational coach who is globally recognized?

I am so tired of an unproductive life—or maybe the lack of love I feel at this moment. It is love that I want so much in my life right now. I have been searching for a certain love for forty-eight years. Why does my life seem so hard and challenging? All the hurts, lies, disrespect, and mental abuse—when will they stop? Why am I going through this right now? Why does everything feel so out-of-sync, so unpeaceful?

I've done really well in bodybuilding and figure competitions, so I really have no plans to compete again. I am tired of that industry and tired of doing competitions. I would rather just stay in shape without the pressure of proving myself in competition. I just want to prove to myself that I can be in great shape at any age—without the approval of others. I just love how I feel when my body is at its best—strong and young-looking, feeling powerful within myself, enjoying how my body transforms into a goddess-like statue. It's euphoric. I haven't felt that way for a very long time, and I am at a point in my life when I just want to be me, myself, and I. I want to be in awe of all the wonderful experiences I will encounter in my life. I always imagined being a very successful businesswoman, helping others and making a difference on earth.

At the age of eight, I would walk down the gravel road and envision myself as rich, happy, and owning my own home and car, and I always felt peace within myself. That successful, passionate businesswoman never worried about where the money would come from. I knew I would feel a rush from my future clients' gratitude, because I would be helping them to make positive changes in their lives. I just wanted people to love me and to be free from my mother's daily beatings. I just wanted to get away from the pain.

I knew, deep down in my tiny little heart, that God and the angels were there for me every step of the way and that there was light at the end of the tunnel, full of peace and love. I walked back to the farm, knowing that my mother was having her "moment," because I could hear her screaming for me at the top her lungs. But I knew that I was growing every day, every month and year, and that one day I could walk away from her and not look back. I would start my peaceful life and love every moment that life presented. I also knew that, once I was away from her and the farm, I would need help to heal all my pain and heartbreak. I knew that there was someone out there who would help me and explain to me that what I had experienced in my childhood was not normal, that I was okay and a good person.

I know I can't change my memories or feelings about being abused by my mother and raped by my cousins. I know that when those feelings present themselves, I need to listen to them and search within myself to discover what triggered them, to feel the emotion and go with it, rather than denying it, to find the message I should learn from it. Many times, I do get the "aha" moment, and I know exactly what needs to be done.

The angels are always with you, and they want you to feel, love, and live for the moment, to let go of the past—as it is only the past—and to feel the present moment, this day, this event, this minute of your life. I know it takes time to feel the moment, and we tend to protect ourselves from any hurt, but it is time to feel the moment and the love in your heart, envisioning the life you have always wanted.

We are all deserving individuals with amazing gifts to share with others. You are a breath of fresh air, an inspiration, a burst of sunshine—and you do make a difference on earth. Love within. Love to feel again. Love love.

Chapter Ten

My Healing Process

AS YOU HAVE BEEN READING my book and letting me share with you what happened to me as a young child, teenager, and woman, you must be wondering what steps and direction I took to move forward in my life and heal myself.

At first, as a young child, I just functioned, day in and day out. I did not know any different, as I thought my life was normal with my mother hitting me every day. I just prayed that my school years would go by fast, because once I graduated, I was home free: no more beatings.

When I look back at my life, I realize that the healing began when I was twenty-five and expecting my second daughter. I was working for a corporate airline company, and the company provided a counseling service. At the time, I felt that I did not need any help, but during my pregnancy, I was having horrible nightmares of the cousins who had raped me when I was very young. In my dreams, they would laugh at me and say, "No one is going to believe you." This went on for weeks. My home life was not any better, as Florence kept working late nights, and if I had an evening shift, well, he had no choice but to stay home and watch our oldest daughter, who was two years old at the time.

In 1987 I finally went to the counselor and asked her questions about her services. She said that the counseling was for people who had personal issues that they would like to deal with in a private setting. No one in the office would know. I didn't want anyone at work to know what was going on in my life. I had to fill out a questionnaire and share with her what I felt I needed help with. Within a few days after our appointment, she made arrangements for me to meet a psychologist in downtown Edmonton.

As I was driving to my appointment, I was thinking, *What will this person have to say to me? Will he or she have a solution for me? Am I really going to finally heal and move forward with my life, or will he or she just provide me with homework or suggestions that I will eventually be disappointed with?*

As I walked into the psychologist's office, I went to the receptionist and said that I had an appointment with one of their doctors. She said to have a seat, that he would be right with me. My first thought was, *Oh my God, it a male psychologist.* I didn't know if I wanted to work with a man, since I had been raped by my cousins and was currently enduring abuse at home. The last thing I wanted was to open my heart up to a male doctor.

He walked toward me and asked me to come into his office. He saw that I was unsure about going into his office or even working with him. As he sat behind his office desk, he could tell that I did not trust him and that I didn't even want to be there. He looked at me and said, "You don't want to be here, do you?, and I said, "No, I really do not want to be here." He then asked me if it was because he was male. I said yes, that I really did not trust him because of what had happened to me and that I did not trust any men, period.

He looked at me and agreed that maybe it would be best for me to work with a female psychologist. He referred me to the sexual assault office, and I agreed. He said he would arrange for that office to contact me to book an appointment. I thanked him, and he wished me all the best.

As I was walking to my car, I felt a sense of relief that finally, maybe, someone could help me heal so I could move on with my life. I had a burning desire to be successful in my life, and I just wanted to move forward and let go of what had happened to me in the past and in my marriage. I just wanted to get my life in order and become the woman I'd always known was inside me.

A few days went by, and I received a phone call from the sexual assault office and booked an appointment with them. Now, this was twenty-five years ago, and all I can remember is that the psychologist's name was Erica and that she was a blessing in my life. She was very soft-spoken, but she really took the time to guide me through what I had experienced at a very young age. She assured me that it was not my fault, that what my cousins had done to me was wrong.

Oh, how a feeling of relief flowed through my body as I talked with Erica, because I had thought that my life was normal and that I'd deserved what my cousins had done to me. Erica had me write a letter to each of the cousins and express to them that what they had done to me was wrong. In the letters I was also to tell them that I forgave them but that I had no interest in being their friend or even their cousin anymore. I wrote Gus and Mitch each a letter, but after I finished writing the letters, I burned them. The burning of the letters sent my thoughts and words into the universe and to God so that they could help me rid my mind of those horrible incidents.

I saw Erica for five years, and what a blessing that was for me, because she was there for me all the time. I recall a couple of very difficult sessions with Erica, times when I had to take further steps, to take responsibility for moving forward and growing.

One step involved contacting the RCMP and making an appointment to report the cousins who had raped me. Erica felt that it was time for the cousins to take responsibility for what they had done to me when I was eight through sixteen years of age. I called the RCMP office in Edmonton and made an appointment to file my report. I went to the RCMP office and met with a police officer who took written notes of what had happened to me when I was very young. He gave me writing paper and asked me to write everything down in detail: where it happened, when it happened, the approximate time it happened, and how old the cousins were at the time of the assault.

At that time in 1987, it had been thirteen years since the rapes. Erica did share with me that when a person has been raped at a very young age her body goes through an amnesia state until she experiences another life challenge. My second pregnancy had triggered the return of my nightmares.

The police officer said to let him know when I was done writing, as his office was just one door down. As I wrote, I remembered a lot of what Mitch and Gus had done to me. I had to give full details of what they had done to me, where it had happened, who had been there when it happened, and how old I was. The memories were stirring up a lot of emotion, but I was driven to get this done, as it was time for me to heal and for them to deal with their own consequences. It took eight pages, both sides, to write the details of what had happened to me. It felt great to finally have a legal document. The police were going to investigate both of the cousins.

I walked to the police officer and gave him my report. He said that they would keep me posted on the investigation and that they would be contacting the cousins for an interview. I shook his hand, thanked him, and walked away. As I sat in my car, I felt as if a huge weight had been taken off my back. I felt so happy that I had gone to report the abuse and that I had the right to do so.

Months went by, and I finally got the phone call I had been waiting for. A police investigator called me at home and shared with me what was going on. He said that my cousins had each hired a lawyer to represent them in regard to my allegations. I started to laugh, as I knew that they were guilty. The officer shared with me what the cousins had said in their reports. I found it quite interesting that they'd said I had made it up and was lying.

I told the detective that if I'd made it up, I would never have gone to the police to accuse the cousins of raping me. I said no, by no means would I have lied to get attention. I told the detective that I was a competitive bodybuilder, and that was my way to get attention—not by accusing my cousins of raping me. He said that the only way we could charge them was if I had semen inside of me to use as DNA evidence. I was shocked that he would say something as stupid as that, as it had been thirteen years ago. There was definitely no semen inside of me. Then he proceeded to say that I had wasted his time and that I should just move on with my life and let it go, as they could not charge the cousins. Then he hung up the phone.

I was so taken aback by his remarks that I got an appointment with Erica the next day and shared with her what had happened. She too was in awe. Erica was wonderful, as she saw that I was quite upset with the detective's remarks. She asked me if I was ready to take the next step to healing, and I said yes. The next step was a big one. She said it was time for me to tell my parents and family.

Well, that was a big step for me, as I had never told anyone other than the airline counselor and Erica. I looked at her in fright, as I did not know if or how my parents would react. Erica suggested that we invite my family to her office so she could be there to support me as I shared what had happened to me. I sat there looking at Erica and decided that it would be best if I spoke to them one by one, and that's what I did.

I called each of my brothers and my only sister and told them what our cousins had done to me when I was eight years old. Then I had a conversation with my father and my mother, individually and face-to-face, to tell them what their nephews had done to me.

My father's reaction was one of surprise, but not really. My mother's response was, "I was hoping that one of my children did not get raped." As she said that, I looked at her with confusion, but I did put the comment in the back of my mind for years. Now I realize that she had abused each one of us in her own way. I really didn't know how to express myself at that time, as I was shocked by each of their remarks. My brothers said, "Well, they did not do anything to me, so I'm still going to stay in contact with them." My little sister was very understanding and hugged me. I do love my little sister. She is very special in my heart.

The following week I had an appointment with Erica and told her what my family had said about my sharing with them what the cousins had done to me. As I told her what each of them had said, she was not surprised. She said that some families do not know how to respond or what to say or do, because when they were young, the way to deal with those sorts of issues was to just brush it under the rug and not say anything to anyone.

As I listened to Erica tell about how people react, I sat there and said to myself, *Now everyone knows, and I am moving on with my life, with or without them. This is my life, and I have started the healing process. I am going to do the best I can with my life and become the woman I always wanted to be.*

I thanked Erica for all her help and guidance, but I had a baby girl at home, and I was in mommy mode. My life was all about the two little girls I was raising at home, and I had to put my own life on hold for a little while. That was fine with me, as I had already done a lot of healing and letting go and could move on with my life.

As the years came and went, I booked appointments with Erica for follow-up sessions, because I was determined to get my life in order. We saw each other for five years in total, and it was the best investment in myself I could have ever made, as that was the beginning of my healing from the past.

As the years continued to fly by, my family and relatives were not very pleasant to me because, of course, families start to talk, and they all blackballed me. Even today, they act like I am a bad disease. What they don't realize is that I don't miss them. I have felt for a long time that maybe the cousins had done the same thing to other female cousins, but no one knew about it. They say you can pick your friends but you can't pick your family. Well, I beg to differ. We can pick our friends *and* our family. Some families are very toxic and disrespectful. You need to do what's best for you, and if that means letting go of close family members, relatives, or friends, then so be it. You need to reclaim your power and take your life back to become the strong individual you always knew you had within yourself.

Take time to heal. Take steps to move forward, because no one is going to do it for you. Don't you think it's time to take responsibility for your life and celebrate the person you are or have become or want to become?

As you read the next chapters, you are going to read of ways that I tried to really heal and let go. It will probably blow your mind, as the process of healing was something I truly enjoyed. To some of you, it may be very new. To others, it may not.

Chapter Eleven

Reconnecting with the Other Half of My Soul

EVEN AS A CHILD, I knew there was something different about me. I always felt disconnected, not whole.

For the past few months, I had not been feeling well. I was always tired and didn't want to be here anymore. I decided to find alternative ways of healing and booked an appointment with an "energy healer."

When I went to my appointment to meet with the energy healer, it was not what I expected. She was a tiny brunette lady, dressed very casually, and her name was Esty. She directed me to her office, which was a very simple room containing two big, comfy leather chairs that faced each other. They were positioned beside a big window, so I was able to look outside and see the beautiful landscape of the Rocky Mountains. There was also a glass of purified water available for me to sip from throughout our three-hour session.

I felt comfortable with her, and I was so ready to heal and let go. We talked for an hour, and she asked me questions about my life, my childhood, my teenage years, and my current adulthood. I was at a point where I needed answers to the *whys* in my life. I needed to understand why I'd been feeling the way I had for such a long time.

Esty coached me into a state of deep meditation. Let me describe what a deep, meditative state feels like. You are sitting in a very quiet place. It's a place where you ask your angels and God to help you allow the healing that must be done. As you are sitting there, you get more relaxed and slip into a deeper feeling of quietness. It feels peaceful and warm. You sense that there is a lot of love around you, and you get a feeling that it is time to start. That's when Esty, or whomever you are working with, starts asking questions like: "Where is your soul?" At first I thought, *What an odd question to ask me*, but I asked the angels to guide me throughout this session.

Esty asked me if my soul was a full soul or half a soul. As I was in a deep, meditative state, I answered that I had half a soul and that the left side of my soul was missing. Then she asked me when I had disconnected myself from that half of the soul. My answer was that I really did not know, because I'd never felt it leave me—or possibly it had never come into this lifetime.

Esty asked me to zone in and go back as far as the day I was born, to see where my soul was. She asked me if I could see myself as a newborn. I said yes, and she asked me where my soul was. I told her it was over my head, not in my body. Esty said, "Okay, let's go beyond that. Let's try to find where your soul was before it came to you in your infant body."

She took me back to my deathbed in my previous life. I was lying in a beautifully crafted oak bed with white bedding. Above the right-hand side of it was an open window with a deep-blue sky and picturesque mountains with snow on the peaks. I had long, flowing, white hair. I was wearing a white cotton gown and was at peace with myself. I sensed that I was a princess and had a very good life.

Esty asked, "Where is your soul?" I said it was with her, the older woman—which was me. Esty told me that when I had died in that lifetime, I had been very happy there. When it had been time to come into my new life, my soul hadn't really been ready for the transition. Esty coached me into deeper meditation and took me into my current mother's womb and asked me what I saw. I said I was curled up on my left side, not happy. I did not like who my mother was going to be, as she would hit me on her tummy. When I saw myself as a newborn, I saw that my soul was over my head.

Esty then asked me to go back to my past life and ask the other half of my soul to come to me. I promised to take care of it and respect it and love it like before. I needed the other half of my soul for this life, so I could continue my life missions. My past self agreed that the other half of my soul would come to me in this life.

Esty coached me in the process of getting back to myself through meditation and then returning to my normal state of mind. As we sat looking at each other after the session, Esty explained to me why I had felt this way for many, many years and why my life had been in such turmoil. It was because I had not been living with a full soul.

After I left the clinic, I was very tired, and my complexion was as white as a ghost. Thank goodness, my husband came with me, as there was no way I was able to drive home. I was so tired that I fell asleep during the drive back home. When we arrived home from my appointment with Esty, I went straight to my bedroom, crawled into bed, and fell asleep. My body and my new, complete soul needed time to settle in, and I needed time to understand what I had just experienced at a very deep, spiritual level in my life.

A few days after my session with Esty, I noticed some changes in my choice of colors in my daily wardrobe. I was now wearing more earth tones and more colors of spring and summer, such as pinks, blues, and purples—and whites, of course.

I looked forward to my next few sessions with Esty, as I couldn't wait to regain the person that I'd truly known was deep within myself. I was not scared to die, as I knew what life was all about, but I did want to finish with this life. I had so much to offer others in this life.

Chapter Twelve

My Second Step to Healing My Whole Soul

I WALKED INTO ESTY'S OFFICE for my second session with her. It had been a week since the first appointment, and Esty looked at me, smiled, and said, "Wow! You look amazing and very beautiful." That was when I realized that my soul was getting stronger.

As we sat in her studio, she asked me if I would like to do a body scan or a cord-cutting. I chose a cord-cutting. I sat in the big, brown, comfy leather chair, and Esty asked me to close my eyes. She spoke to me in a very gentle and soothing way to get me focused in a meditative state. Coaching me to relax, she asked me whom I would like to start with, and I said, "My dad."

I was in a state of deep meditation, and she brought me to a visualization of my dad standing in front of me. She asked if my dad and I were connected. I could only see that my throat was attached to my father's throat. Esty coached me through a process of "cutting the cord" and asked Archangel Michael to assist me. Esty asked me if my father was upset when I asked him to let me go. I said that he was not. He understood why I was doing the cord-cutting, and he approved. I was then asked to send a white light to surround my father, which represented my love and forgiveness, and I asked Archangel Michael to escort my dad away to the white light.

Let me explain the white light so that you all understand what I mean. When I am in a deep meditative state, I visualize white wings hugging people with love. It may be Archangel Michael who presents himself to me in a silhouette as a strong male figure, and I can sense that he takes care of them. He helps them cross over to a better, more blessed life, whether they are alive today or have already passed away.

The next person I approached was my abusive mother. She was attached to me at both of my shoulders, both elbows, and the back of my head. Esty instructed me to do the same process we had done with my dad. I asked my mother to let me go, and I said that she must move on without me. At first my mother refused to let me go, as she felt that she was in charge of me. I asked Archangel Michael to help me cut all the cords that bound us. Esty then asked me to surround my mother with white light, indicating that I had forgiven her and that I loved her. We were done. I saw Archangel Michael cutting the cords from her and wrapping his wings around her as he escorted her out. Finally, I did not see or sense her anymore.

After that, I visualized my little sister. It was funny, as my sister popped up right in front of me. We were holding hands, and our hearts were attached to each other. Esty again coached me to ask my sister to let me go, telling her that everything would be fine. My little sister smiled at me and had no problems letting me go. As she was walking away with Archangel Michael, she was blowing me kisses. I said *I love you* and surrounded her with white light. As Archangel Michael was taking her away from me, I had tears coming down my face, but they were tears of happiness, as I knew she would always be in my life.

The next person I addressed was my brother, who is fourteen months younger than I am. He stood in front of me with his arms crossed and a scowl on his face. As I looked at him, I noticed that we were connected to each other at our elbows and hips. When I asked my brother to let me go, he looked at me with a frown and let me go with a hissy attitude, saying, "Okay, fine. Do whatever you wish. It's your life anyway." I asked Archangel Michael to cut any remaining cords and to embrace him with white light, and then he escorted my brother away.

After him came my youngest brother. It was interesting but not surprising to find that he had me at my throat and my left hip and wouldn't let me go. Esty asked me if he was letting me go, and I said no. She then asked me to tell him that I needed to move on and so did he, that he did not have permission to stay attached to me. It only took a few minutes, but it felt like twenty to thirty minutes before he finally allowed Archangel Michael to cut the cords. I asked for white light to surround him as he left.

My middle brother was next, and he was attached to me at my head and elbows. I asked him to let me go, and at first he said no, but with Archangel Michael embracing him, he let me go and left with white light surrounding him as well.

The next one was my cousin Mitch, who had raped me when I was eight years old. He was choking me with both of his hands and was attached to me at my hips and my tummy. Esty coached me to tell Mitch to let me go, that I wanted my life back, and that he should move on as well. At first he refused, but Archangel Michael and Archangel Raphael came and cut all the cords that were attached to me. I asked for white light to surround him, and Archangel Michael escorted him out into the white light.

The next confrontation was the toughest, because Esty felt that I was getting too tired to continue. She asked me if I wanted to continue. Although I was tired, I just wanted to get this healing done so that the next session would be a new healing process for me. I told Esty I was fine and asked her to continue.

That was when my second cousin, Gus, who had raped me, came to me. He was attached to my forehead, both hands, elbows, and knees. I told Gus that he needed to let me go, that it had been too long, and that he couldn't hurt me anymore. He would not let me go.

Esty sensed that Gus was not letting me go. She then asked me to ask Archangel Michael and Archangel Raphael to help me cut the cords with Gus. We were able to cut the cords binding my head, my elbows, and my hands, but for the life of me, he would not let go of my knees. It felt like we were bound by a cable and that there was no way he would let me go. Esty asked if he was letting go, and I said no. I did not tell Esty where the attachment was, but she bent over and literally broke off the final cord that connected us.

As soon as Esty had severed the cord that had connected us, I felt a draining feeling down the right side of my head and body, like water was draining out. I told this to Esty, and she said, "Good." She asked me to come back into my body and to wake up slowly and get re-grounded. I agreed, as I felt very tired. I slowly woke up, opened my eyes, and gathered my thoughts. As I sat there in my big, brown, comfy leather chair looking at Esty, it felt like everything was in 3D. It was quite interesting, and it really did not scare me at all.

Once, I was fully awake, Esty told me that, with everything I had been through in my life, I should have died, but something was keeping me here to finish my life mission. I knew what she meant by her remark. All the years of abuse, disrespect, and bullying—from family members, my ex-husband, relatives, and schoolmates, in the workplace or the bodybuilding world—had been a constant in my life. That day, I was at peace with my life. I knew that I was not a bad person, but I had been through a lot. I now knew that when I pursued my own business of healing coaching, I was going to help those who had experienced some of the same issues that I had experienced in my forty-nine years. She said that by the time we were done with our sessions, my life mission and my passions would be of service to others in this wonderful world. My purpose would present itself, and I would continue to heal within myself for the rest of this lifetime.

As Esty was walking me out of the studio, she said that in our next session we would continue cord-cutting with the cousin who had raped me, and with other family members who had treated me—and still treated me—with disrespect. I was so tired from my session with Esty, but I knew that it had to be done so I could move on with my life mission. I accepted it and looked forward to all the new life challenges and adventures that were going to be both positive and fulfilling.

Chapter Thirteen

Letting Go of My Family in a Spiritual Way

THAT MORNING IT WAS WARM and peaceful, and I was looking forward to working with Esty and finishing the last bit of cord-cutting. As I sat in Esty's office in my comfy, brown leather chair, facing her, she asked me how I felt after our previous session two weeks ago. I shared with her that it felt like a huge weight had come off my shoulders, and that I had no attachments of anger with my mother or the cousins who had raped me.

Esty began our session like always, by getting me in a comfortable state of deep meditation, so that we could finish the cord-cutting session that morning. As she spoke to me and got me to relax, she asked who was standing in front of me. I said it was Gus again. She asked what he was doing. I told her that he was standing in front of me with his arms crossed. He was refusing to let me go, as he was attached to my heart.

Esty told me to ask Gus why was he having such a hard time letting me go. Gus answered that he owned me and that he could do whatever he wanted with me. I started to laugh at him and said that I had heard that before. My ex-husband Florence had said the same thing to me when he was served with his divorce papers.

I told Esty what Gus had said, and she asked me to ask Archangel Michael to assist me in cutting the cord that connected our hearts, to ask Archangel Raphael to surround Gus with white healing light, and then to walk away, accompanied by both archangels. At first, as always, he refuses, but with the help of my angels and my telling him that he must move on, he eventually let go and was escorted away by my angels with love. When I could no longer see him, I told Esty that Gus was finally gone.

Esty asked me if I was ready to cut the cords from my children and other family members, and I said yes. So we started working on my first daughter, May. I called out for May, and she came to me and hugged and cuddled my legs, with her head on my lap. I said to May that I was going to cut the cord between us in an energetic way, that I adored her, and that everything was fine. Esty asked me to put a white light around her and to send her love, which I did. I visualized May surrounded by white light and sent her love, and then she left.

The next daughter was Marie. It was interesting, as she was attached to me on the right side of my body and was very angry with me. I asked her to detach herself from me energetically, as I needed to take care of myself and heal. Marie refused. As I was in my meditative state, Esty could tell from my facial expression that something was going on between Marie and I. I told her that Marie was refusing to let me go. Esty asked me to let Marie know that I would always love her and would be in her life for a very long time. Instead I told Marie that I did not agree with how she was currently living her life and that she knew what I meant.

Marie nodded her head, and we embraced with love. Then I told her that I was cutting the cord from her but that I would always be in her life and that I loved her so very much. Archangel Raphael then hugged Marie and walked away with her. As she was looking back at me, I blew her a kiss to let her know everything would be fine and to assure her that I truly did love her. After she left with Archangel Raphael, I started to cry and had a hard time breathing. It was so hard on me, letting my girls go, but I understood that it was an emotional release of energy and was not permanent. Once I'd settled down, I felt much better and was ready to continue my session.

Esty then called on Rose, my third daughter, and she came to me. Being a bit of a goof, she danced and laughed all the way over, not paying attention. Esty asked me if I felt any kind of attachment, and I said no. She then asked me to surround Rose with white light and to tell her that I loved her very much. Rose then left with Archangel Michael cuddling her with his wings and walking her to the white light.

Next came my last daughter, Isabella, who was seven years old. Esty asked me if there were any cords attached to me from Isabella, and I said no. She asked if I was ready to let her go, and I said no, as I felt she was too young right then and that she still needed me. Esty agreed and asked me to surround her with white light and to let her know that I loved her very much. Isabella then went with Archangel Michael.

The next person was my ex-husband Florence. Esty asked me if I could see him, and I said yes. She then asked where we were attached, and I said, "At both knees, the back of my head, and both hands." Esty asked me to let Florence know that it was now time for him to let me go and leave, as our marriage had ended long ago. At first he did not want to let me go, even though we had been divorced in 2002. Esty asked me to tell Florence that he must go on with his life and that I wished him all the best. Finally he let me go, and I embraced him with white light and said good-bye.

Next was my current husband, Anthony. As he was walking toward me, both of his hands were tucked into his pants pockets, which I felt was quite interesting. Esty asked me what was going on, and I shared with her what I saw in Anthony. She said to embrace him with white light and to say that I loved him and wished him well, and then he left with Archangel Michael. The whole process took an hour and a half, from start to finish. I was tired, but I felt amazingly peaceful.

Esty coached me to come out of my meditation, and we talked about Marie, as Esty had felt my daughter's anger as well. Esty said and that we needed to work with Marie energetically through me so that she too could heal. Esty felt that Marie had perhaps brought something into this life from her previous one. She asked me how my pregnancy had been, and I told her that I had been very sick for seven months while pregnant with Marie. Esty felt that once we worked on me and looked into what had happened in Marie's past life, it would help both Marie and me to let go and move on in a loving and positive way. I stood up and gave Esty a big hug and thanked her again for her healing.

For the next three days, my legs ached badly, and I had a very hard time standing. The pain interfered with my sleep, as it continued to bother me at night.

I would have to ask Esty at my next session why my legs were so sore Until the next session, *à bientôt*.

Chapter Fourteen

Another Way to Heal: Visual Body-Scanning

TODAY'S SESSION WAS VERY INTERESTING, as I found out that, with my complete soul, I am a different person with different feelings. As I looked into the mirror this morning, I saw a different me—a whole *new* me. I had a session this morning with Esty, and we worked on scanning my body parts to clear up particular areas of my past lives. As I am journaling my experiences, I tend to forget the areas, but I am going to do my best with my angel's assistance.

As always, we started with my taking a deep breath to get me into a calm state of mind to prepare me for my session in a meditative state. When I was ready, I let Esty know by a nod of my head. Esty started to scan my body to see where we needed to start releasing some body blockage. For example, my right arm often went numb as I slept at night—to the point where I couldn't feel it. This woke me up, and then I would shake my arm and move my fingers to bring back the circulation to my right arm.

As I sat in Esty's comfy leather chair, she asked me when this numbness in my right arm started, and what caused the pain. As I sat there, I got a vision and told Esty that it was not from this lifetime. She asked me to take my soul to where the pain had begun. I saw that in my past life I had been a princess in Europe, and a knight had been ordered to take me to the forest and kill me. He had tied my hands together and walked me to the forest.

When we arrived at the location in the forest, the knight asked me to get on my knees and look away. As I looked away, he took a big, flat, wide type of bat and hit the right side of my head. I fell to the ground and felt blood streaming down my head and flowing down the right side of my face. I tried to get up, but the knight followed his orders and hit me again. As I lay there on the ground, he turned me over to see if I was dead. Then he began to choke me to make sure I was dead. He left me in the forest. My body was left there to decompose into the earth.

Esty told me to ask my soul to leave my dead body completely. She said to ask if my soul was okay with the way it had died. It said no. It felt that she should have had a proper funeral to say good-bye. Esty told me to ask my soul what type of proper good-bye she would have preferred: a burial or something else. My soul said cremation, so I visualized my soul completely leaving my dead body as it was burning. I visualized my body lying on a bed made from tree branches. I was wearing a full-length, white, cotton dress, and it was burning. I watched it burn until my body was total consumed. I asked my soul if it was satisfied with the final good-bye, and it said yes, it was the proper way to leave.

Esty told me to ask the soul to come back to me and heal my right arm with white light. It came back to me in this life. A jolt went through my right arm, and I felt a tingle. It felt great—alive and strong again. I find it very interesting that I can go back into my past lives and experience how I died.

In one previous past life, I had been killed as a princess because of a war at that time. I had lived in a castle, deep in a forest that was part of that past life. In the life I'd lived just before my current one, I had been a princess again, but I had lived in a castle in the Alps. In that life, I'd lived a life of luxury, but what I found most interesting was that I had been a smoker—a heavy smoker—and had eaten very well, my favorite food being white cheese. I knew these things because we were scanning my lungs, which felt congested and unhealthy. It felt like a typical smoker's unhealthy lungs, and I had a hard time breathing properly.

We then went to another area of my body: my right kidney. It had a bit of a gray area, and I shared that with Esty. She said to ask my soul why my right kidney was so unhealthy? I asked my soul, and the answer was that I had eaten a lot of white cheese in my past life before this one. I found that quite interesting, as I didn't smoke in my present life, and I didn't really care for any kind of white cheese. I occasionally had wine and cheese at the odd time or event, but that amount was no comparison to my past life.

We also worked on my ovaries, as I'd had a miscarriage in 2003 when I was eleven weeks into my pregnancy. It had been a baby boy, and its soul was still with me, as it was scared to leave me. Esty asked me to talk to the baby boy's soul, which I did with Archangel Michael's assistance. I told my baby boy's soul that everything would be all right and that it was okay to leave with my angels, as they would take very good care of him. I told the baby's soul that I loved him and that we were going to meet again, but for now he must cross over and heal with Archangel Michael, who would take very good care of him. I cuddled him with my angels. The angels and I gave my son a kiss and said *I love you*, and then they left. I started to cry, as the son I'd always wanted was gone. He was off to a better place, and I truly believe that we will meet again with love.

After that, Esty brought me back, as my session was done for the day. I told Esty about the day I had miscarried my baby boy, and I said that I could not understand why it had happened to me. I'd had no problems getting pregnant with the first three babies. Why had it happened with this baby, the son I'd always wanted? I had been depressed, feeling that I had failed my husband, Anthony. He did not have children, and I had wanted to keep his family name going for the next generation, as he was the only male left in his family. I had felt empty within, alone and very sad. I had spoken to a lot of women who had lost babies through miscarriage and had learned that one in four women miscarried. I finally felt peace within myself, believing that there was nothing wrong with me and that God had plans for my son. Two months later, we were blessed again, and I was expecting a child. Oh, how blessed I felt to be given a second chance to bring a baby into our lives.

We talked for a while, and I shared with Esty how different I felt. Lately I'd felt that I wanted to leave earth. She said that the earth and universe were going through a major shift and that I was not alone with those feelings. Many people were waking up and asking themselves,

What is my purpose in this life? Do I end it now, or do I continue with this life and complete my mission of healing?

Esty shared with me that her guides felt that I had much more to give and that I was needed on this earth to complete my healing before I could move on to my next life. I agreed with her, as I was just getting to know my whole soul, and it would not have been fair to me, my new, complete soul, or Isabella to end my life. I had so much more to offer in the coming days, weeks, months, and years. By the end of my life, I was going to know who I was, and I would be fully healed. I was getting stronger with every session with Esty, and I looked forward to future sessions. I would seek her help in later years as the need arose.

Although you are reading about my life experiences, I know that some of you won't "get it," as they involve very deep spiritual healing. Then again, some of you will be able to relate. I embrace my new soul, my life, and whatever presents itself to me in the coming days, weeks, months, and years. If I can help others to heal and to empower themselves to take charge of their own lives and take steps to heal, then I have made a difference in their lives as well as mine.

We can do so much good in other peoples lives, but only when they are ready. I cannot force you to take the next step in your life to heal, as this is something you need to do for yourself. When you are ready, I am here to guide you and to celebrate your life, your soul, and the person you have always known yourself to be.

Until next time: love, respect, and embrace.

Chapter Fifteen

Healing from My Second Pregnancy

TODAY'S SESSION WAS ABOUT HELPING me to understand my daughter Marie and the body-scanning of my second pregnancy. Of all my pregnancies, the second child was the hardest on my body. I was sick for seven months, but I was working shift work part-time, which gave me enough days off. On the days I was home with morning sickness, I was able to rest and get ready for work. At times I would get up in the morning and only be able to eat crackers. They were the only food I was able to keep down. I thought, *Oh well, every pregnancy is different*, but this pregnancy was most definitely a daily challenge for me. Since I was working with Esty in a spiritual way, it was not about how every pregnancy was related. It was deeper than that.

In this session, Esty prepared me for a meditative state. She coached me to see why Marie was reacting the way she was in her life today—and why I had been so sick for those seven months before having her. Marie was currently living a very destructive lifestyle, and I had not spoken to her in ten months. Was I concerned? Yes, I was!

You might be asking yourself why I did not contact her or go to see her at work or at home. It's because I felt she needed time to find herself without my saving her all the time. Her biological father was not helping her at that time, as his way of helping her was to keep her dependent on him by giving her money whenever she needed it. Rather, he should have encouraged her to take responsibility for her own life, to go out and get a job and create the life she'd always wanted. My way of helping Marie heal her life was through Esty's spiritual coaching.

Esty coached me to relax and to ask my angels to come and guide me so we could get started with the healing. By this appointment, I had no problem getting into a meditative state, as my body and my mind were getting accustomed to the routine. I called each of my angels—Archangel Michael, Archangel Raphael, and Jesus—to help me heal and forgive myself, to love myself throughout this session. Once I sensed their presence, I let Esty know.

We began on the night that Marie was conceived, a warm summer evening and the same evening that Florence had assaulted me in front of my cousin from Ottawa. That evening, Florence had rolled himself over me and said that I deserved it and that no one would ever support me—just as my mother had not defended me that morning. That night Florence also said to me that he was the man of the house and what he said was law. I had no voice in this marriage. I was so emotionally tuned-out that I felt nothing but emptiness.

I recall that I lay there that night as he did his manly thing to me. I was not on any kind of birth control, as he would not allow it, preaching to me that if I was on the birth control pill, it would be a sin. I was so numb from life and living with half a soul that I believed him.

Esty took me to the night that Marie was conceived and asked me if Marie had come with a full soul or half of a soul. I sensed only half a soul, a sad soul. I told Esty what I'd felt and envisioned, and what Esty shared with me made sense. She said that Marie's spirit had been attracted to my sadness and had come into this life with her own sadness and half a soul as well. Her spirit had come to me because I was sad and lonely, and she attached herself to me.

Esty then proceeded to go through every month of my pregnancy, asking what I was feeling from the spirit that was grieving inside of me. Every month, from the first month to the seventh month, I was sick. The baby's spirit was sad that I was not happy to be expecting her at that time because of my personal life, my marriage from hell, and a husband who had no intention of loving me or respecting me as his wife. My husband forced himself on me for sex, never considering how I felt or how the baby growing inside me felt. I was always tired, sick, and in a loveless relationship. Before getting pregnant, I had considered leaving him and raising my first daughter alone—without his help and away from his abuse toward me and my daughter May.

Esty got me to the seventh month of my pregnancy, which was the first month that I finally felt better health-wise, because that was when I finally accepted the pregnancy. I felt I had no choice but to move forward and love this gift of life and be its mother, just as I did with my first daughter. Esty asked me if the spirit of the child was still sad, and I sensed that she was not, that she was accepting the fact that she had made a choice and was coming into this life to heal.

In the eighth and ninth months, the baby was getting ready to be delivered. I recall that on the morning she was delivered the doctor had to induce me because the baby's heart rate was going down and there was concern for her safety. Esty asked me if Marie had cried after she was born. When Marie came out, she had barely cried—not like her sister who had come out crying, letting us know she was there. Marie had been a very good baby. Within three weeks, she slept through the nights, had a very good, healthy appetite, was very quiet, and had a very kind soul. When Marie began to speak at the age of two, she had a very deep voice, but it was very gentle in her own way.

Esty shared with me that Marie had been in the same situation that I was in when I came into this lifetime as half a soul. The way she was acting up in this life was understandable. The drugs, partying, lack of communication with me, and living a destructive life were all part of having only half a soul. We asked the angels if Marie was ready to heal, and they said no, but I believe that in time she will be. Esty asked that, every night before I went to bed, I send Marie white light to surround her and her son with love so that they could be healed and protected. Then I woke up from my meditative state.

Since that appointment, I am more at peace with myself and Marie. She was not a reflection of my mothering but of what had happened to her spiritually when her spirit had been attracted to my loneliness and sadness. I know that one day Marie and I are going to have a heart-to-heart chat, and I will be able to reach out to her and help her heal herself—but only when she is ready to do so.

I love you, Marie, and when you are ready to do what I am doing and reclaim your full soul, I am going to stand by you and watch you become the person, the woman, you should have been from the start when you came into this life. You are a loving, kind, and beautiful soul. I can't wait for that day. Love and happiness await you, Marie.

Je t'aime,
Maman

Chapter Sixteen

Fifty-Plus Years to Make a Difference

AT TIMES I FIND IT very interesting how people I know or meet can—or cannot—relate to me. I have worked so hard on myself to better my life and heal within.

I had to start from the point of being a child raised by an abusive mother. Day after day, she did her best to beat me down, to crush my soul and my personality so that she could feel that she was better than me and could control all aspects of my life. She was basically a sick controller who thought that what she did to me and our family was acceptable. She always spoke down to me, even when I was in grade school. She purposely did not take time to help any of us on our homework. It was like she wanted to make sure that we were inferior to her. She did not want any of us to become successful in our grades or to do well in school or even to attempt to attend any college or university.

My mother was very good about celebrating the successes of the other kids she taught at our school, as it made her look like an awesome teacher. What the others did not realize was that my mother was very abusive to us in our home in her own sick way. Maybe the other teachers at school knew that she was not a very nice mother to her own children, but as long she didn't hit *their* children, who really cared? When I was younger, I recall that my mother shared stories about other parents giving her permission to punish their children if they misbehaved.

She told us that when she taught fifth grade—I was just a baby at the time—she had forty-five students in her class, and one of her students was my cousin Gus, the one who later raped me when I was nine. She said that Gus would not listen to her, even though she was both his teacher and his auntie. She, of course, had a short temper, so she grabbed him by his ear, pulled him away from his desk, and threw him to the floor—to give the other students a message not to mess around with her, or else. That was how she was at home, beating us with her whip, leaving marks on our tiny little bums and telling us, "I hope you learned your lesson. I am your mother, and you'd better listen to me, or else." That was how our lives were. We were living with a very destructive woman on a power trip.

My only sister, now a grown woman, shared with me that she too had been hit by our mother. I asked her when it had begun, and she told me it was when I moved out of the house in the summer of 1980 to go to college. As I sat there, listening to her story of how she had been abused by my mother and my brothers, I felt her sorrow, because I could relate to her. Now I understood why she had been so over-the-top when she was fourteen years old—so mean, so out of control. At that time, I had asked myself what the heck was going on at home and in her life. I had been away from home for a year. She was only ten years old when I left for college, and at that time, our way of communicating was by writing to each other. Phone calls at that time were expensive, so we did not talk very often on the phone.

After our conversation that evening, I realized that my sister was still mad at me, because I was her only sister, the oldest of the family, and she had needed me to protect her. I had not protected her at that time because I was focused on college and was dealing with my own insecurities. All that time, I had thought that my mother was abusing only me, but in reality she was abusing all of us in her own secretive way.

I have always wondered what my mother did to our brothers, because today, as grown men, they are verbally abusive and very hot-tempered. Our father was not hot-tempered at all, and he had a good heart and soul. So, really, our mother must have done something to them to make them the men they are today. I've always wondered about it, but they are living their own lives, and it is not up to me to help them out. I have tried to suggest that help is available, but they have always laughed at me like I was from another world. I always spoke the truth to them, and that was when they became abusive to me with their language.

At times I also wondered what happened to our mother when she was a little girl. She did say that her mother did not treat her well because of the size of her own family. Her family consisted of sixteen siblings and four adopted children. Life in those days was simple, but the economy was booming in the forties and fifties. It is said that parents use their own upbringing to raise their children, because they think their own experience was normal. Had my mother's mother abused her when she was a young girl? Had my mother herself been belittled? I guess I will never know, as my mother has changed very little, even today.

She is currently going through a divorce from my father, as she has decided that she wants out of their marriage after forty-five years. The biggest problem is the way in which she is going about it. It is unacceptable as she has involved my brothers, nieces, nephews, and her grandchildren. Let me share with you what I have witnessed.

Five years ago, my mother came to my house in tears and "cried wolf" about how my dad was abusing her. I found this quite interesting, as he had never, ever abused us in any way. She shared with me that she wanted out, because my father did not want to retire from farming, and she felt that it was time for him to retire so that they could travel the world. She assumed that I would take her side. I had already been through a divorce, and she knew how hard it had been on me, having been treated unfairly in the final papers. Unfortunately, I did not call my father and listen to his side. I believed her story. I shared with her what I had experienced as a settlement, and I stated to her that she was entitled to half of everything he had.

She stayed for a few days at my home and then left to live with my brother in Red Deer. She floated from one brother to another, until she decided to purchase a motor home to live in. I knew exactly what her intentions were: for people to feel sorry for her and believe that my father was mean to her. She wanted everyone to believe that she had no choice but to purchase a home on wheels.

What people don't know is that my father had written a check for her to purchase a condo in Red Deer, on which she had put an offer. But she refused his check. My father had been willing to pay for her condo outright. The facts were completely different from my mother's story that he had refused to pay. She ran and cried to every family member that my father had not been faithful and had refused to give her money. My father had been more than generous with my brothers, helping them out with any of their farming issues, lending them equipment or giving advice. But then they wanted more.

I know that my father, once he passes away, has a plan in place that will help my sister and me, but it's not about how much he gives us. It's about the relationship I have with him, and his relationship with my daughters and my husband. I am so grateful to him for him helping me and loving me. He is an amazing, gentle soul, but for years people have taken him for granted, not giving him the respect he truly deserves. He does have his closest friends, and he has me and my daughters who adore him.

The other grandchildren are also caught up in my mother's web of greed and lies. She really does not consider the consequences of what she says, and she is determined to make my father's life miserable, because she wants his money. My father shares with me that certain grandchildren disrespect him and think it's okay that they insult him with rude remarks. The sisters-in-law are no better, as they feel that their opinions concerning my father's farming methods are much better than anything he has done.

One sister-in-law told me that the only way to keep my father from visiting his son, my brother, at their farm was to cook spicy food, which my father dislikes very much, so that he doesn't come back. My husband heard the story firsthand while visiting their farm one summer and relayed it to me.

Do my brothers appreciate their father's help when it comes to running the combine in the fall? I always wonder. My father gave them each two quarters of land, and my father loves to work the land. My understanding is that when you work the land, prepare it for seeding, seed it, spray it, harvest it, and then sell the grain at the seed plants, you get paid for your grain. Really, my brothers should appreciate what my father has given them: a legacy of financial freedom. Am I bitter? No. It's my father's farming business, and what he wants to do with his legacy is his business, his choice. I wish my brothers all the best in their lives, and I hope they really appreciate the gift my father has given them.

As for my mother, I truly believe that she has mental health issues in that she abuses anyone who does not support her vision. Some people she knows are creating stories that are untrue, even though they know how mean she can be and how she can lose her temper. She has gotten wound up to the point that she threatened to kill a cousin of mine for breaking up her marriage, which was untrue. When I heard that, I spoke to my cousin about it. She shared with me what had happened, and I believed her. I told her that if my mother ever threatened her life again, I would support her, and she should call the cops and have her arrested.

At the end of the day, people don't understand that when they disrespect and threaten people or try to destroy their lives, the tables eventually turn on them, and their own personal lives are affected. For example, their health is adversely affected, their circle of friends turns against them, their marriage falls apart because of greed, and so on. Many people who were very disrespectful to their spouse or family have ended up alone and broke financially. I have seen it happen.

I have fifty-plus years to go in this lifetime, I am going to constantly keep working on myself to heal my heart, to really connect within myself, as I know that when my time comes and God comes to get me, I am going to be totally healed from my life lessons. We are all on this earth to learn and heal every day from the life lessons that we did not learn in our past lives. We are here for a reason. I know that my next life will be amazing, and I have asked God, my angels, and my guides to make my life a very positive experience. I wish for my mother Barbara to come back in her next life and make positive changes so that she does not bring her vindictive ways with her. I wish for her to heal and become a kind, gentle soul.

I had an angel reading once, and they shared with me that what my mother is doing to all of us today is something she brought with her from her past life—the greed, the vindictiveness. She was supposed to have changed in this lifetime, to better herself and heal, but that didn't happen, as she has done nothing but hurt everyone in her own sick way. Maybe in the next lifetime she will grow up and take responsibility for her actions, but I won't be there to view that.

I love my father very much, as he is a very kind soul, and I have learned much from him regarding the dos and don'ts in life. When it is his time to go and he has completed what he needed to do in this lifetime, God and his angels and guides will come to get their child, and I know he will be well taken care of.

Yes, life has been interesting for me, with lots of life challenges and disappointments, but I have also had a lot of great fun, and I have always analyzed every situation to understand why it happened—in either a negative or positive way. After falling down, I've always gotten back up, because I know something better is yet to come, and I need to learn something from it. At times this was hard on my heart and soul, but I had to learn something and move forward. I know that there is a light at the end of the tunnel in every aspect of my life. That is why, when my daughters call me and say they are having "moments" in their own lives, I am able to hear what they say and guide them to realize the importance of the life lessons they are currently dealing with. As well, I am working with my daughters, stressing the importance of keeping their families close to them. I remind them to love, respect, and support each other mentally, physically, emotionally, and spiritually, as they are valuable human beings. They are all amazingly gifted women, and we are all connected in spirit. They know that I am there for them, no matter what. My daughters know that, even when I am gone, I am with them and my grandchildren in spirit, that they can call on me in spirit and I will come to them and help them. We are all energies, and we can sense our past family members by our sides. Some of us will understand this, but others . . . well, they are so disconnected from life that they just don't get it.

I have been blessed with an amazing gift from God and the angels. When I have "one of those days," I am able to channel to my angels, my guides, and God, as they are there to help me by giving me signs—a feather, a coin, or a bird landing next to me—reminding me that I am loved. Everything will work out for a better life, whether it be financial, emotional, or both.

Today, people need to value themselves more and stop running around with their heads cut off. It is time for you to take responsibility for your life and to change your ways. If you are not happy, life is not working for you. It's okay to change in a positive way, and only you can do it. No one can change it for you. Accountability with yourself is the first step. Take baby steps to heal within yourself. Make decisions as to what you want in your life: better health, a better career, and better quality friends. You don't need a large quantity of friends—just really good *quality*. True friends value your friendship rather than judging you or telling you what you can or can't do.

You need to work on yourself—moment by moment, minute by minute, hour by hour, every day—because only you can be you for the better. I have survived, and in the next fifty years I want to make a difference in people's lives, to help them heal and to guide them toward being the best they can be. I value people for who they are, and I want to work with those who are looking for help in healing. I am always working on myself, and I will continue, right to the day that God comes to get me.

Value yourself, as you are the most beautiful, amazing spirit that God has created. Start grounding yourself and stop bouncing around, as it is affecting you in all aspects of life. Take time for yourself, and don't be too concerned about what people think: at the end of the day, it's really none of their business.

Chapter Seventeen

Sedona: Let the Healing Begin

ONE MORNING WHILE SITTING AT the kitchen table, I was drinking my coffee and trying to wake up, as I had not slept well the night before. I kept thinking to myself, *When is this feeling of being angry about my life ever going to end?* I had made an appointment to meet that morning with Allyson, who is my angel reader. I needed her help and guidance so I could figure out how to let go of this built-up anger my body was holding onto. I was tired of getting up in the morning with all this unwanted chatter in my head—thoughts of people who disrespected me and unhappiness with the way I looked or felt. You know the saying: *I am sick and tired of being sick and tired.*

In my session with Allyson, my angels would provide me with the answers I was waiting to hear through Allyson's reading. Allyson could sense and see how tired I was. I was not my bubbly self. The look on my face showed that I was exhausted. My body was slouched over, and I had no energy to sit up straight. As Allyson pulled out one card at a time, she displayed each one on the table between us. One particular card came out, and it was the healing card. We both looked at each other, as we knew that I had to do something about my health.

Allyson shared with me a message from the angels: "Google retreats." That evening, after all of my daughters had gone to bed, I went on my computer and Googled "retreats." I was surprised. I had not realized that there were so many different retreats that catered to all different types of healing. There was one particular retreat in Sedona, Arizona, that drew my immediate attention and kept coming up. It was time for me to heal and to let go of my inner anger. The retreat website had a free monthly newsletter that I could sign up for. I thought to myself that I had nothing to lose, as I was still searching for the right retreat that would suit my individual needs.

The next morning, I turned on my computer and checked my e-mail. I noticed that I had received an e-mail from the website where I'd signed up the previous night. I opened the e-mail and started to read about Sedona, Arizona. This company catered to people who were in transition, who needed to take control of their lives and take steps to heal inwardly. I read the whole newsletter and then deleted it, as I felt that maybe the retreat would not be able to heal my anger.

Three days later, I received another e-mail about the retreat in Sedona, and this time it had a different message. It highlighted previous clients who had attended the retreat and talked about how it had made a difference in their daily lives and how they had become different people. The retreat had really saved them. I read the stories and felt that maybe this could be the retreat for me, but of course my self-talk kicked in, and I decided to delete the e-mail again.

Two days later, I opened my e-mails, and there was another message from Sedona. This e-mail suggested that I call the office to see if they had a package that would suit me. They would work with me to find a package that suited my budget. I grabbed the phone and contacted the company in Sedona. The phone rang, and a nice lady answered my call. She asked how she could help me. I mentioned my name and shared with her how I'd found out about the company and had signed up for their newsletter.

She asked me, "How many times did you delete our e-mails?"

I started to laugh and said, "Three times." She started to laugh as well. She asked what had stopped me from deleting the last e-mail. I told her that I felt that maybe their company would be able to help me with a healing package that would suit my needs and my budget. She asked if I had a few minutes to answer some questions, and I said I did.

She asked me what goals I had set myself for going forward. I shared with her that I was ready to heal myself and was looking for a way to let go of the anger that I was carrying within me. I shared with her that my angels, through my angel reader, had directed me to go to a retreat to heal.

She asked me if I had ever been to Sedona, Arizona, and I said no, as I was from Calgary, Alberta, Canada. When she was done asking me a few more questions, she said she would call me back in twenty minutes with a package that would suit my needs and budget. After our conversation, I thought to myself that she would probably call me the next day, as I felt it must take time to design the right package for each person they spoke to. With all the anger I needed to heal, I was sure it would take some time to work out a plan.

Well, the phone rang exactly twenty minutes after our conversation, and a lady named Mary asked to speak to me. Mary said that she had two different packages for me. The first package was wonderful and very appealing, as it had certain elements of healing that interested me, but it was way too expensive for me. The second package she proposed to me was okay, but it had only a few healing sessions, and that did not appeal to me at all. However, it was within my budget. She asked me if I liked the second package. I said yes, but there were several sessions that I felt would not be a good fit for me. We talked about the two packages—what I liked and what I disliked about each one. As we talked, we came up with a custom package that suited my needs and my budget. After that, Mary sent me the proposed package via e-mail. I signed it and purchased the package.

I was burning with joy inside, because I had never done a retreat or been to Sedona, Arizona. Two months later, I was flying to Phoenix, Arizona, with my husband Anthony and Isabella, as I wanted my family to experience Sedona with me. As we drove to Sedona, the scenery was absolutely beautiful. The mountains had deep reds and brown colors, and cacti were everywhere in the countryside.

When we arrived in Sedona, I was in awe of the red-stone mountains and the calm that was exuded by the town itself. We arrived at the condo I had rented for us, and we unpacked the car and settled in for the evening.

The next morning, I had an appointment with the retreat company at nine o'clock. I was very tired from our flight and the drive the night before. As I was getting ready to go, I walked out onto our back deck, and the views I saw were amazing. I thought our Rocky Mountains in Canada were breathtaking, but these mountains were a deep red and brown. The sky was a crisp blue, and there was a calm, warm breeze.

Anthony and Isabella came outside and just couldn't believe how beautiful Sedona was. Isabella looked up at me and asked when were we moving there. I looked at Anthony and said, "Maybe one day." She did not understand that we were not in Canada anymore but in the United States.

I got myself ready for my day and then drove off in our rental car to my appointment. Being from the big city, I thought I should leave a half hour before my appointment to give myself enough time to find the office.

When I arrived at the office, I looked at my watch and realized that it had only taken me ten minutes to get there. I started to laugh to myself, as I realized that Sedona was a small town with a population of maybe fifteen thousand—unlike Calgary, which has approximately one million people. I assumed that most of my appointments were probably going to be very close to each other, so I wouldn't have to leave extra early because of the traffic—which in Sedona was quite light.

I sat in my car to kill some time, as I did not want to go in too early for my appointment. Closer to my appointment time, I walked into the office. A lady with blonde, shoulder-length hair came toward me and said, "You must be Angelique." She gave me a heartfelt hug that I hadn't felt from anyone in a very long time. At first I resisted, and then something came over me and told me to allow the hug, as it was time for me to let go and let God take care of me.

The woman's name was Debra, and she asked me to have a seat. Vince was to come and get me, as he was my first appointment and my guide to show me Sedona. She explained to me that Vince would go through my itinerary and tell me what to expect on their three-day retreat.

Finally, Vince came in. He was a tall, slender man in his mid-thirties, and he shook my hand and welcomed me to Sedona Soul Adventure Retreat. As we sat in his office, he explained to me that we were going to take a drive so he could show me where each of my appointments was. I gave him a surprised look and said, "Oh! I thought that all of my sessions would be at this location." He looked at me with a smile and said no.

My session with Vince was called Orientation and Power Spot Meditation. He said, "After your orientation, we will go to one of the energy vortex spots and do a meditation session so you can connect with earth energies and set your intentions for your time here in Sedona. This will be a time when you literally "plug into" the earth's energies." He explained to me that each session would be at an individual healer's home office.

Off we went to our first location at one of the spiritual vortexes in Sedona. It was a location I could visit if I wanted to go to it on my own time to meditate. When we got there, I saw that the landscape was basically hills and unique trees that had their own distinct look. They were not like the normal trees I saw every day in my own area. The tree branches were not really straight; they had unique bends and curves to them. The leaves were a turquoise color with silver tips, and green cacti were everywhere.

Vince took me to a location not far from my car, where there was a valley with trees, cliffs, and a small creek running through it. We sat on the edge of the cliff, which was not very high, as I am scared of heights. Vince shared with me that he was my first coaching session and that he would guide me through a meditation session. I had no clue about how to meditate. I mentioned to Vince that I had never experienced meditation. He shared with me that it was like closing my eyes and praying to my God or "source." He asked me to close my eyes, relax, listen to the wind blowing in my ears, and allow God and the angels to enter into me.

As I was sitting on the edge of the cliff, I sensed my body getting calmer. I felt a peace within me, and then my body started to swirl with the momentum of the vortex. Let me describe what it felt like. A vortex is like a circular funnel with a wide opening at the top, and it tapers down to the point of the funnel. My body was swirling round and round with the momentum, and I felt like I was moving in a circular manner. At times my body would go really fast, and then it would slow down. I knew I was connected with the vortex and the universe.

Vince said he would coach me over the next three days and that I was going to heal my inner self. He said I should enjoy all the healing sessions planned for me and embrace the call of all the wonderful blessings that would come my way during the sessions. He said that all the healing teachers I would meet were looking out for my best interest.

Vince said that when I was ready I should open my eyes, as my session with him was done. I opened my eyes and immediately noticed that the landscape of trees, flowers, and hillside were much more vibrant in color than they had been before our session. The leaves were a turquoise color, and each leaf had a silver outline to it. The cactus flowers were vibrant with bright colors—like pinks mixed with yellows and reds. The hillside colors were a more prominent brown, with a touch of deep reds engraved in the rocks. I felt like the blowing wind was singing to me that I was safe and that everything inside me would be healed.

Vince gave me his hand to help me get up, and we walked toward my car, as we still had a few more places to go to. He took me to another area in Sedona where I could view a double sunset in the evening. He explained that the mountains were in a line and that the reflection of the moon gave an illusion of a double sunset. He said that the best time to view the double sunset would be a few minutes before 8:00 p.m. and that I should experience that with my family.

We walked back to my car, and I drove Vince back to his office. I had another appointment scheduled, and I needed time to look at the map they provided so that I knew how to get to each appointment.

I arrived at my next appointment with an "intuitive reader," the second of three appointments scheduled for that day. I parked my car in front of the intuitive reader's home, and of course I was ten minutes early. I sat in my car to take a moment for myself, to get mentally ready for this appointment.

Let me briefly explain "intuitive reading" for those of you who have never heard of or experienced it. During this time I was to be connected with a gifted psychic and given answers to my questions, information about who I really was, and information from my angels and guides.

Angelique E. Constance

I took a deep breath and opened my car door to go to the house. As I was walking toward the house, the door opened, and standing in front of me was a beautiful brunette woman with shoulder-length hair, who said to me, "I have been waiting for you." I smiled and walked into her home. I introduced myself, and she walked me to the table where she had her own personal tarot cards laid out for my reading.

We sat down at the table, and she began taping our session, as I was only booked for an hour with her. She shared with me insights of what was going on in my life, that it was time for me to be in Sedona to heal my past, and that the best was yet to come. She told me that I had been a healer in my past lives and that I was going to help people heal themselves in this lifetime. There were lots of people who had experienced the same life challenges that I experienced as a child, teenager, and adult, and I had much to give. I knew that I was going to make a difference in the lives of both women and men.

After she completed my intuitive reading, I thanked her, and off I went to my last appointment of the day. This session was called "Release the Pain and Grief." As I was driving to that appointment, the road became very narrow and winding and finally came to an end. I was surprised, but I took a moment to look at the address again, to make sure I was at the right place. As I was reading the directions, I heard the angels say, *Look quickly to your right.*

At first I paused, and then I looked to my right. There she was, standing in front of a little cottage, looking at me with a pleasant smile. She was a very tall, slender woman with long, black hair pulled to the right side of her head, and she wore a long, violet dress. She looked like a princess from a past life.

I got out of my car and introduced myself, and she introduced herself as well. Her name was Brigit. She walked me to her studio, which was set apart from her home. When I walked into her studio, I saw that it was very simply decorated with a massage table to the right. On the floor to my left were all different kinds of pillows in all shapes and colors.

Brigit took me to the pillow area first and asked me to sit in the middle of them. I sat there with all these pillows surrounding me. She then put a large pillow behind my back so that I would sit upright. She explained to me that her focus for me was to release all the pain and grief I had experienced until that day. She asked me to tell her about my childhood experiences and my teen years—all the way through adulthood.

I shared with her about my mother, about being raped by the cousins, and about the abuse I had tolerated most of my life from my mother, family, and ex-husband. She asked me to close my eyes and just focus on my breathing to prepare me for our session.

She began coaching me to go back in my life to where the abuse had started. I went back as far as I remembered, which was five years old. She then asked me about the little girl within me and how she felt. I said she was very sad, and she just wanted her mommy to stop spanking her. Brigit asked me to go back to the little girl within me, as she was going to help me heal and not to be so angry. The little girl within me smiled and thanked me for protecting her. Once I sensed she was gone, I began crying. At the time, I did not fully understand why.

Brigit explained to me that because my mother had abused me so much at a very young age, I had closed up. I had put up a high wall around me, as I was protecting myself from feeling the pain that my mother was inflicting upon me. But the walls I had erected for my own protection had closed in that little girl within me as well. The tears were a result of finally opening myself up and allowing the little girl within me to resurface and to feel my heart and soul again.

As I was in my meditative state, Brigit also asked my inner child to help me grieve and let go, as it was time for us to get to know each other again and to forgive our abusive mother for what she had done to us. Our mother's angels and guides would work with her to help her heal. I took a deep breath and let it all go to the universe.

Brigit asked me to open my eyes and then asked how I was feeling. I told her that I had a huge headache but that I finally felt at peace with myself. As I got up from the floor, I felt a little light-headed, and Brigit took me to her massage table to do some body-talk energy-releasing to help my body heal. As I lay there, she spoke to my body intuitively and ran her left hand across my body to sense where the blockage was, which she removed energetically from my body. I thought to myself, *What the heck is she doing?*, but my body was responding to it, and I could feel the warmth from her left hand as it removed the blockage I had been holding onto all those years.

Once she felt that I was cleared, she touched my right shoulder and said that our session was done. I got up from the massage table, and she walked me out of her studio to my car. As I drove away, I thought about my session with Brigit and realized that she had not spoken very much throughout our session. I found that very interesting: a healer with a gift that could help heal people with very few words.

I arrived at the condo. Anthony and Isabella had been watching television while waiting for me to return. Anthony asked me how my day had gone, and all I could say was, "It was interesting, and I am emotionally exhausted." I looked at Anthony and said I needed to take a nap for half an hour before going out for supper. He agreed, as he could see that I looked exhausted and very pale.

When I woke up from my nap, I felt refreshed, but I was not the same person I had been that morning. I felt that the blanket of anger had finally left me. A load of anger and grief was gone.

Here is a brief explanation of my last session of the day. Grief, anger, frustration, guilt, fear, and similar emotions keep us from living the life of connection and happiness that we are seeking. In that session, I was taken on a journey to connect with my emotions in a safe, nonjudgmental way. I released these and other challenging emotions in a way that moved them out of me safely and completely, allowing that space to be filled with a greater connection with the source or God—and ultimately myself.

Chapter Eighteen

Sedona: Understanding the Past Life

THE NEXT MORNING, WHICH WAS day two of my retreat, I again had three appointments scheduled with three different healers. My first morning appointment was with an "inner journey" healer, who concentrated on breathing and sound healing. As I arrived at this healer's home, I knocked on the door and heard a faint voice telling me to come in. I walked into her simply decorated home, and on the floor was a bed made of pillows. On the right was a statue of Buddha.

As I was looking at the home décor, a tall, slender, blonde woman came up to me from her outside garden and asked me to join her. She introduced herself as Yanna. As we sat across from each other, we chatted, and she shared with me what our session would be all about, asking me to allow the healing experience to take place.

Yanna told me that she would be using a simple, special breathing technique in conjunction with sound healing. She explained that I would enter an altered state. I would experience the movement of energy, the release of blockages, and a direct connection with the source, God, and the divine—in physical, mental, emotional, and spiritual ways. The last half hour she would spend in integration. She asked me if I was ready to let go and allow God to take the next steps to my healing, and I said yes. We went back into her home, and she brought me to the area where she was going to conduct our session.

In that area were pillows, a single futon bed, and a Buddha statue next to the place where I was going to lie down. As I lay down, Yanna put a round pillow underneath my legs to support my lower back. She provided me with a pad to cover my eyes, as we needed to get me into a deep meditative state, and she wanted my body to think that the room was completely dark. Yanna then covered me with a blanket, as it was an hour-long session and she wanted me to be comfortable.

As I lay on the futon, getting ready for my healing session, she explained to me that she would be playing music behind my head. The music was specially designed for the type of sound healing that I was going to experience. She started the music.

The first song had sounds of wind, flowing water, and an Australian music pipe instrument. It had such a nice rhythm to it that I wanted to get up from the floor and start dancing, as my heart and soul loved the feeling of the song. Yanna asked me to breathe to the beat of the music that was playing. She instructed me to take a very deep breath and then let it out slowly, exhaling to the point where I was completely exhausted and I needed to take another deep breath. She wanted me to get connected with my spiritual self. I felt at peace within myself, and I felt I was floating with each breath and song that presented itself.

From time to time, Yanna would speak to me with her soft voice to allow the healing, to allow the visions that were being presented to me. With each different song she played, I felt I was traveling to my past lives all over the world. During the first song, I had a vision that I was the descendant of an aboriginal native of Australia. With the second song, I felt that I was in Africa. The third song made me feel that I was dancing around a fire with people from my tribe.

The forth song was intense; I felt that I was dancing with a group of women in a place where I lived as an Egyptian princess. I saw that my eyes were outlined with black eye pencil. I looked very mysterious, and I could hypnotize people with my eyes. I was wearing a headpiece with a black veil that covered my whole face but had an opening for me to see through. I had a gold chain tied across my forehead. I sensed that I had a very blessed life as a princess in Egypt. All I could see in my vision was that I was dancing and having a lot of fun with other princesses from the palace.

The next song was a flowing music, and it took me to a place where I was a very well-respected princess in India. I had a vision of being a Hindu princess who had spiritual healing powers. The villagers would come to me for healing and were grateful for my healing powers. I was much respected in that lifetime.

My body and soul were taking me through every one of my past life experiences, showing me who I was and how blessed and gifted I was. With each life, my soul enjoyed all the healing I was experiencing as I let go of each past life. I was in such a deep meditative state that I finally felt at peace and for the first time in my life. I was not concerned about where I was, what was happening, or who was around me. I was totally within my spirit and soul, allowing every transition with each song that presented itself.

The next group of songs had sounds, and the message I received from them was to let go of all the anger within me. I needed to let go of my fears and disappointments, as what I had experienced in this life had not been intended to be so harsh. Life was supposed to be loving and peaceful.

My body was moving all over the bed. My legs were sore, and my arms felt tingly. I could not stop bouncing all over. I felt like I was releasing all the blockages, all the things that I had closed off in myself. I was finally releasing all the abuse I had encountered.

Yanna spoke to me with a soft voice and told me to allow the healing. She said that my body was letting go of the blockages that I had been holding on to for many years. Spiritual energies were flowing throughout my body and connecting with my soul and God. As soon she said to let it go, my body settled down. When I had a tendency to hold my breath, she coached me to breathe, as it was through the constant breathing that the release occurred through my body and soul.

The next song began to play, and it was a very powerful song, I must say. It took me to a place that seemed to be in Rome. I was a male warrior with a strong, muscular build, getting ready to fight in a war for my kingdom. I had a team of warriors who honored me and were loyal to my leadership, as they listened to my commands. We fought in this kingdom war, and I saw my warriors fighting for their king. It was a very harsh war, with many of my men dying, but we were determined to win for our kingdom.

I saw myself fighting with my sword. My right arm was cut by another warrior's sword, and I was bleeding. We believed that we were defending our country, and I was on a mission to win. We fought fiercely and won the war, and we carried our injured warriors back to the palace.

With the next song, my vision came to me really fast, and I started to cry, totally out of control. I couldn't believe how I felt—so sad, my sorrowful heart in deep pain. I was standing on the edge of a high, steep hill, facing my palace door and holding a child in front of me. It was a girl with brunette, shoulder-length hair, around six to eight years old. I was dressed in a long, soft, flowing, mauve dress that went right to the ground and had a belt around my waist. My hair was pulled to one side, and it was long and flowing and very black.

I was standing there with my daughter in front of me, looking out over the cliff with tears running down my cheeks, as my only son had been taken away from me. I felt my daughter's pain, and I began to struggle with our sadness, knowing that we would never see my son again.

Then suddenly the vision was gone. I began to cry uncontrollably, as if someone dear to my heart had passed away. It had been a very long time since I had cried that hard. Yanna spoke to me to settle me down, and she got me to breathe again, as the next song was about healing and moving on with my inner soul's healing. I felt a peaceful sense of enlightenment and celebration of life come over me. My soul and spirit had been waiting for me to feel free, to celebrate, to find peace of mind.

My heart finally felt light, energized, without the heaviness I had been experiencing or carrying for forty-seven years. Oh! How I was rejoicing within myself and enjoying every transition from this inner sound and breathing session. I did not want the session to end, but I knew that it was coming to an end for now. I knew that more healing needed to be done. As I was breathing deeply in and out, my body totally relaxed. I said to myself, "Oh my! I wonder how I am going to look when this session is done." That morning I had worn makeup and mascara—which wasn't waterproof. Oh well. Who cared?

When the next song began, I was at peace with myself and was allowing the healing to present itself, as this was about letting go of my anger and the people who had come into my life with the intention of taking my power of self-worth from me. I could sense my body being rejuvenated, and I felt my self-worth presenting itself. My heart and soul were feeling energized, refreshed, less encumbered, and at peace.

The last song I heard that day still affects me today. Even as I am writing this, I am crying as I share my feelings and visions. I saw myself at my own funeral.

I was dressed in a white, cotton gown, and my hair was very long and white, like snow. My daughter May was standing at the head of my coffin, looking down at me. She was sad, honored, and grateful to have had me in her life, knowing that I had been the best mother I could be for her and her little family. Rose and Isabella were embracing each other with tears in their eyes as they stood at the right side of my coffin, reflecting on all the support I had given to both of them in their life's mission.

My only son-in-law, Frederick, was standing beside his wife May with his hand on her shoulder for support. Marie was at the foot of my coffin, looking at me with a big smile of gratitude, feeling blessed to have had a mother who loved both her and Patrick unconditionally. At that point, while I was lying on the futon, bawling, I knew deep in my heart that that day would come in my lifetime.

My funeral appeared to have been held in Sedona. While I was lying in my coffin, my soul and spirit at peace, a vision came to me. I was outside of a peach-colored stucco house with the Sedona mountains in the background. The skies were a crisp blue, and the morning sun was beaming on all of us. I felt and sensed the gratitude of my daughters and grandchildren. It was a celebration of the goodness and blessings I had bestowed on others in an attempt to be of service and to empower women and men with my business, Mother Earth, and the Lord Jesus. I was at peace within myself that day, and I knew that even when I was gone, I would always be there for my daughters and grandchildren in spirit.

I also had another vision. I saw May, Marie, Rose, and Isabella in Kimberley, British Columbia, after my funeral at May's log home. They were sitting on the porch talking about me and sharing with each other the life lessons they had learned from me, remembering how I had always been there for each of them.

Marie and May were hugging each other and crying. Rose was holding Isabella's hand, and they were looking at each other with tears running down their cheeks. Rose wiped her eyes and then wiped her little sister Isabella's tears away and said, "Maman always told us that we would have each other, that we would to be there for each other, no matter what. We are family, and families support each other and respect each other."

May, Marie, Rose, and Isabella got up and hugged each other in a group hug and said, "We love you, Maman." As they were holding each other's hands, they began dancing in a circle. It was a sort of celebration of their mother, and they knew that I was there watching them dance with joy.

As they were dancing, a little girl appeared on the left side of my body. She had dark brown hair and was about five years old. She came to me and held my hand. I asked the angels who she was, and the angels said she was Isabella's future daughter. I started to laugh and said to the angel that Isabella had always told me she would never have children. I looked at the little girl who was my future granddaughter and said, "Isabella will be an amazing mother to you," and she looked up at me and smiled.

At this point, Yanna started speaking to bring me slowly back to the present. She told me to take my time getting up, as she felt I had done some major energy healing and releasing. I needed time to regroup. Once I felt that I was grounded and ready to get up, I removed the eye-covering from my eyes. I pulled my mirror from my purse to check myself out. Oh my! I had mascara all over my eyes and cheeks. I looked like I had done a bad makeup job on myself. I wiped my eyes and cheeks with a tissue so I would look a little more presentable when I left to meet my family.

Yanna helped me to get up and asked me to come outside to her garden to have a conversation about our session. She wanted to know what I had experienced throughout the sound and breathing healing session.

I told Yanna how certain songs had affected me and shared with her about my different past-life visions. I said that each song had had a profound message and that I had been healed from each vision. She asked me about one particular part toward the end. What vision had I been sensing? she wondered.

I shared with her that I had been at my own funeral and that my family had been celebrating my life and saying their good-byes. I asked Yanna why I had seen my own funeral. What was the message there?

She told me that it indicated a new beginning, the start of a new life, which meant that I was moving on and letting go of my past and present life. New beginnings, new ventures, new friends, and new opportunities were going to present themselves to me now. The friends and family members who were currently in my life were going to move on, because they would have a hard time with the new me. I was done with them, as I had learned what I didn't want in my life from friends or family members. I knew which friends and family members I had already pulled away from.

Yanna said that my vibrations were so beyond theirs that they didn't mesh with mine anymore. She was so right, and I was at peace with myself. As long as I had my daughters in my life, that was all that really mattered to me.

I thanked Yanna for this most amazing, blessed experience, gave her a heartfelt hug, and left for my next appointment. At that point, I was ready for my "nurturing massage." Oh, yeah! It would be a delightful, restful time for me.

I arrived at my appointment for my massage, and the massage person was waiting for me on her porch. She introduced herself as Michelle, walked me into her little studio, and asked me to get undressed for my session.

She left the room and gave me a few minutes to get undressed and to lie down on her massage table with a blanket that she provided to cover up and keep warm. As she began working on me, I literally fell into a deep sleep. That one-hour session just blew right by. Michelle had to wake me up, as I was in a very deep sleep. I got up, got dressed, and left for the condo, as I still had one more session, which was to be held at my condo.

Anthony and Isabella were out, checking out Sedona and spending quality time together as father and daughter. I checked my watch and saw that I had fifteen minutes to rest before my next appointment. I lay down on my bed, exhausted from my first appointment, and fell into a deep sleep again.

The doorbell rang, which woke me up from my sleep. I got up from my bed and went to open the front door. Standing in front of me was a tall, full-figured woman with long, curly, dark hair. An amazing energy presence exuded from her. She introduced herself as Tony.

I welcomed her into my condo and walked her to the kitchen table. We sat across from each other, and she explained to me what our session would entail. It was called "spiritual astrology," and she explained to me what it was all about. She said it was very different from traditional Western astrology, in that it focused on one's life purpose and soul mission. It would also produce information on lessons my soul was working on and major cycles I was working through in my life.

Tony pulled out the spiritual astrology portfolio that she had worked on for me and shared what she had found out about me and what my messages were. As we sat there, she described more of my past lives. In one of them, I had been a wizard—a very good one. Kings from different countries came and sought me out for guidance. She said that I'd had a wife and children but that I had been very busy being of service to the kings. When people took advantage of me, I would get upset and zap them into a bug or whatever creature came to mind. This sent a strong message to all who would seek me out: *Do not mock me.* Sometimes I changed people's bodies. The rationale was for me to have fun—and to scare them so they knew not to mess around with me. Eventually I would change them back to their human forms.

Tony said that I had been a warrior in another one of my lives. I had been in great shape and was a great warrior, a great fighter. I'd fought in wars for my country, and I had been very loyal to my band of warriors as well. She said that I had been killed by a rival warrior because of a lie from another warrior who had wanted to take my place as the chief warrior for the king, and it was my king who ordered my death.

After my life experience as a warrior, my spirit decided to become a woman in the next life. Tony shared with me that I had come from royalty, and money was never an issue for me. She also shared that I was a very strong, educated woman who always did well for herself.

As Tony went through my astrology chart, she found it interesting that I had come into this life to heal my past. In this life, my mother was not the mother I'd had in past lives. I'd had to learn from this mother what kind of parent I wanted to be—and didn't want to be. This indicated that I was a late bloomer in my career in this life because of all the personal challenges I had experienced with abusive individuals. She said that doors were opening to opportunities in all aspects of my life, and greatness was yet to come—with health, wealth, and happiness.

Tony shared things with me about my daughters and the baby I'd lost five years earlier. She explained why I had lost my son in this lifetime. She told me that in one of my past lives I had been a princess with two children, a daughter and a son. War had erupted in my kingdom, and one night the enemy kingdom sent soldiers to my castle and kidnapped my son. They took all the sons in my kingdom as punishment. Now I had daughters and no sons because of that previous life experience in losing my son from that life. This explained the sadness I'd experienced after the loss of my son in my kingdom.

When Tony reached a particular area of my chart, she stopped and started to laugh. She said, "Hi, Mom," as she looked at me. I looked at her in a quizzical way, and she explained to me the numbers on my chart and what they represented. Our numbers matched, and this meant that we were related. I had been her mother in some form in a past life, and she had been my daughter. We laughed, and she finished our appointment. I walked her to my door, paused, and then gave her a heartfelt hug and thanked her for her services.

To be honest with you, I did sense a connection with her the moment I opened the front door. It felt like we had some sort of connection from a long time ago. It is said that when you meet someone and feel an instant connection, you knew each other in a life before this one. I truly enjoyed her reading, as it brought clarity to my understanding of why I am the woman I am today—strong, in shape, driven, persistent, and passionate. I'm finally understanding and getting connected with my intuitive gift as a medium.

Anthony and Isabella came in and asked how my day had gone. I shared with Anthony about my day, and as he was listening to me, he said he had noticed a huge change in me over the past few days, as I was calmer and more at peace with myself. At that moment, I knew I'd made the right decision to come to Sedona to heal myself.

The next morning was my last retreat day in Sedona, and I thanked God that I only had two scheduled sessions for that day. I'd already had two intense days that involved major healing and releasing blockages from my body and soul. I was quite tired from all of my sessions with the healers.

My morning session on the third day with another healer was called "Soul Source Union with Ranjita." As I looked at my map and drove to her home, I noticed that it was on the outskirts of Sedona. I had asked Anthony to drive me to my appointment, as there was a tourist attraction down the way from this healer's home. It was a natural slide in a creek that had been formed centuries ago. I'd thought it would be fun for Isabella, as she loved the waterslides in all the hotels we'd stayed in. Because it was in the mountains with natural waters and great mountain views, I thought it would be a fun and unique experience.

My husband drove me to this healer's home, which was on a very narrow country road. The views were beautiful, with vistas of Sedona, amazing red-stone mountains, and landscapes full of cacti, trees, and flowers on both sides of the road. As we arrived at the healer's home, I looked up to see where she lived. Her house was positioned on the hill. It looked like it was built right into the hillside. We parked our car, and as we walked toward the home, a beautiful, slender, organic, blonde woman walked toward us and introduced herself as Ranjita.

She showed us a huge rock that had fallen from the mountainside a week before our session. It had landed beside her home and in front of her rose garden. I looked at this huge, red rock and noticed that it was in the shape of a heart. Even Isabella remarked to Ranjita that the big, red rock looked like a big, red heart. Ranjita smiled and explained that the gods from the mountains and Mother Earth had sent this heart-shaped rock to her home with a message that she is loved and that everyone who comes to her for healing is going to be blessed through her services. She gave Isabella a hand-sized piece of the heart-shaped rock, which had chipped off from the main rock when it fell beside her home. Anthony and Isabella left for their waterslide experience in the mountains.

Ranjita took me into her office studio, which had a massage table facing a big window with a mountain view. I could easily see the huge, heart-shaped rock resting at the side of the house with the roses in front of it, looking like it had always been there. She explained to me what our session would entail.

A Soul Source Union healer was a type of practitioner who was very gifted at guiding people into the depths of their being through the use of guided imagery and symbols. She would assist me in reconnecting with all of the "lost" parts of myself.

In this session, she would facilitate my reclaiming of my essence and the parts of me that were intuitive, innocent, trusting, and connected with my spirit. This was a very powerful process for ensuring transformation on all levels—physically, mentally, emotionally, and spiritually. It was really a process of taking me into the highest part of myself.

Ranjita asked me to lie down on her massage table with my feet facing toward Mother Earth of the Sedona mountains. She covered me with a blanket to keep me warm during our healing session. She covered my eyes with a meditation eye cover that had a lavender scent to it. She started playing very soothing, peaceful meditation music, which had a nice, flowing, musical tone to it. As I lay there, she started to speak to me to get me into a meditative mental state. She had me breathe deeply to get me into that zone.

Soon I felt my body quiet itself, and I entered a peaceful mind-set. All my brain chatter was gone, and I knew I was ready to allow the next and final healing session to work its magic. Ranjita asked me to find my inner little girl, to go deep within myself and ask my guides and Archangel Michael to assist me in finding the little girl within me. I asked my body and soul to guide me to locate her.

At first my body and soul would not respond to me. It felt like a very high brick wall was in front of me. It was so high that I couldn't see the top of it. Ranjita asked me what was I seeing. I told her how high the brick wall was. She asked me to ask my body and soul why this wall was so high. I asked my body and soul, "Why is the wall so high?" My body and soul answered, "We are protecting our little girl, because she's been hurt so many times in this lifetime."

Ranjita asked me what my body and soul had said, and I told her exactly what the vision had said. She said to let them know that I was the grown-up little girl that they had been protecting all these years, that I wanted and needed to meet my inner little girl, as it was time for me to heal and to be with myself. My body and soul agreed that it was time, as my inner little girl has been very lonely.

Ranjita asked me to visually start breaking down the brick wall, one brick at a time. At first it was really tough to break through, but as I persisted, the bricks began to break down, one by one, until finally the whole wall collapsed. Ranjita said to ask the little girl who she was. I asked the little girl, "Who are you?" She said, "I'm Angelique." I told Ranjita what the little's girl name was and mentioned to her that it was me, Angelique.

Ranjita said to ask the little girl if she would like to have parents to protect her and take care of her, and I did. She said, yes. Ranjita asked me to ask Archangel Michael to bring my inner little girl's parents to protect her and take care of her.

In my meditative state, I saw a male come to me. He was wearing a long, brown coat that covered him. He looked like one of the men from medieval times, as he had a small rope tied around his waist as his belt. He had blonde, wavy, shoulder-length hair and a beard. He was holding a cane in his right hand as he walked toward me. I asked his name, and he said he was Joseph. I turned to my inner little girl and asked her if Joseph would be the perfect father for her, and she said yes.

Ranjita then coached me to ask Archangel Michael to bring my inner little girl a mother. At that point, a beautiful woman walked toward me and my inner little girl. She had long brown hair pulled back into a ponytail and was wearing a long, mauve dress with a brown shawl resting across her shoulders. I asked for her name, and she said she was Jemalia. She had such a warm, loving smile.

As I looked down at my inner little girl, I asked her if she was pleased with our new mother, and she said yes and smiled. Jemalia and Joseph came toward me and told me that they would take good care of my inner little girl and that they would love her like one of their own. I smiled at them and I gave my inner little girl a hug and told her that her new parents were going to love her as if it were the first day of her life. I would always love her too and would be there for her always. She smiled, and Jemalia and Joseph each held a hand of my inner little girl. I told them I was very grateful to them for protecting my inner little girl. They both smiled at me and said they loved me too. Then they all walked into the distance to their new home.

At that moment, I started to cry, realizing that what my own mother had done to me as a child, making me close myself off from life, had been very cruel on her part. She did not have permission to take away my childhood and crush my innocence. As a little girl, all I'd wanted was to be happy and to venture out and experience the wonderful world I was living in.

Ranjita sensed that I was very upset with my mother for all the cruel things she had done to me. She asked me to forgive my mother, as my mother also had childhood secrets that she needed to heal from. I was to let it go and let God take care of my mother. She needed to resolve her own life lessons on her own, and I was not responsible for her life.

As the music kept playing, Ranjita asked me what I was seeing. I shared with her that I saw my friend Charles. Charles was with other angels, and they had surrounded me. I shared with her that Charles had come up to me, put his arms around me, and given me a heartfelt hug full of love and respect. He told me that I was safe and loved and that he would be with me always. He mentioned to me that I had so much to give in this life, that it was not my time to leave to join him. He said that I had a mission to go out into this beautiful world and share my story with others, as they needed me to help them heal and to take back their power to live. He said there was a greatness waiting for them, but they needed my help to take the steps to achieve their own personal life goals. I smiled and agreed with Charles.

Suddenly, as I was telling Ranjita what Charles had said to me, I saw this white energy, full of intense love, peace, and happiness. It was a very calming feeling. This energy surrounded Archangel Michael and all the other angels as it came toward me.

Ranjita asked me who else was with Charles, and I told her what I was seeing. Suddenly the intense white energy came to me as Jesus. I was in awe that I had finally met Jesus, as he had protected me since the day I was raped by my cousin at the farm. It was the most beautiful feeling I have ever experienced, and I felt very blessed, as it gave me peace and a confirmation to keep going in my life's mission.

Ranjita told me that I was surrounded with a lot of love, respect, and happiness, and that these individuals were just letting me know that they were there for me always. I started to cry with relief. It was a confirmation to me that the angels, Jesus, and Archangel Michael had always been by my side from day one. My dearest friend Charles had always been there for me when he was alive, and now I had the pleasure of having him in my life in spirit. I finally felt loved and knew that I would never be alone.

Ranjita started to speak to me in a very calm voice to prepare me to get regrounded, as our session was almost completed. After I slowly woke up from my intense meditative state, I lay there looking up at the ceiling. I felt refreshed and at peace within myself. The anger I had been carrying all those years had finally left me. The heavy chest feelings and the headaches were gone. I smiled and thanked the Lord Jesus for being with me. I asked that he never let me give up and that I would always see a light at the end of the tunnel to a better, more fulfilling life.

I got off the massage table and wiped my eyes again. It had been another amazingly intense healing session. Ranjita asked me how I felt. I shared with her that I felt different, at peace, with no heaviness in my chest and no headache. I felt that I had been reborn again. She said that my inner little girl was back within me and that I needed to go out and play again, to rejoice in my new life, as there was so much for me to venture into and experience.

As she walked me to my car, Anthony and Isabella were waiting for me. Ranjita gave me a book with two CDs in it. The CDs contained music for me to use to meditate and to reground myself when I got back home to Canada. She shared with me that I was going to be more sensitive and more intuitive. I had released a lot of the anger within me, and now the next chapter of my life was going to present itself.

I was a healer, and the work I was going to pursue would be based on healing others. I had been through so much as a child, a teenager, and now a woman. There were lots of women in this beautiful world who felt that they were alone and saw no way out of their current situations. I would help them to come out and rejoice, to be the women they had always known existed within themselves.

Ranjita gave me a heartfelt hug, which seemed to be a common experience with all the healers I had worked with in those three days. They sure loved to hug.

I thanked Ranjita for the beautiful healing experience.

As we were driving back to our condo, I asked Anthony if he could take me to the Chapel of Holy Cross, which was on a vortex as well. It was built into the red rocks of Sedona. As we arrived at the location, I saw that it was the most beautiful Roman Catholic church I had ever seen. It was built into the red-rock mountains and had a walkway that went right up the hillside and into the church. As we walked up the winding pathway, I felt a peace within myself that I hadn't felt in my life. I felt a love within myself that I had never experienced until that day.

As I walked into the little church and sat in a pew, I said a prayer to Jesus and the angels, thanking them for giving me a second chance in life and for making a difference in my life. I thanked them for all the blessings and healing that I had experienced in the three days I'd been there, and I was grateful to have a newfound peace within. I thanked Jesus for all the messages he had sent me in respect to faith. I knew that my life would be blessed and that my disappointments were going to be lifted. I apologized to Jesus for not acting sooner. Then I took a deep breath and thanked Jesus, my guides, and my guardian angels for being there for me always.

As I walked out of the hillside church, Isabella grabbed my hand to show me something she had found. She took me to the edge of the pathway and said, "Look, Maman. On the side of the red-rock mountain. It's Jesus's face." I looked and asked her where. She pointed at the mountain that was facing us. She pointed out to me the side profile of Jesus's image. She pointed out the crown that he had worn when he died on the cross for our sins. She pointed out his eyes, his cheeks, and his mouth.

I looked down at Isabella with a smile and said, "Yes, I do see it." And we hugged. She then said, "Maman, Jesus loves us." And I said to Isabella, "Yes, he does." I looked up at my husband Anthony and smiled. We took a picture of Jesus's face on the hillside of the red-rock mountain and left to go back to our car.

As I reflected back on the three powerful healing days in Sedona, I knew that my old, angry self was gone. I also recognized that the new me was very welcome, and I was embracing that. My healers did say that when I got back home, I might lose a lot of my girlfriends and family members, as they would see that I was a changed woman. They wouldn't understand the new me, and they might push me away. To be honest with you, I was fine with that.

A few days later, I saw my daughters, May, Marie, and Rose. All three of them noticed my transformation into a much calmer, more peaceful and loving mother. They shared with me that I was not an angry person anymore, that I didn't wear a frown on my face, and that I did not look upset all the time. I told my daughters about my experience in Sedona, about all the healers that I had worked with and what each session had done to help me let go of the inner anger that I had been carrying all those years.

I also mentioned to my daughters that we needed to make a trip to Sedona so they could look at these healing retreats for themselves. I felt that they too needed to do some healing within, to rid themselves of the accumulated garbage in their personal lives. It was time for my daughters to let go and let God take care of their healing, as I knew that my divorce had had a personal effect on them as well.

As you are reading this chapter, I know that deep within you, you want to make positive changes in your own life. Maybe it is time for you to take the steps that I have taken, as they have helped me immensely—to heal, to let go, to pursue the life you've always wanted. I truly believe that all the diseases out there in this world are based on the emotions that we have held on to for years. Maybe you don't realize that there are alternative ways that can help you to let go and be healed within. When we are in difficult situations in our personal lives, we may feel that no one understands us and that there really are no solutions for us to heal our hearts.

Being in the health industry for thirty years, I have seen men and women struggling with their weight and self-worth. I know for a fact that when you take the first step and say, "Enough is enough," and act on the belief that there are alternatives for healing within, then you are going to empower yourself. As a woman or man, you have always known within yourself that you are an amazing, beautiful soul, and the weight will come off, just knowing that. I believe that the extra weight you might be carrying is from the emotional baggage you have experienced in your personal life, not realizing that it is a partial cause of your weight gain.

We tend to complicate our personal goals, whether they involve weight loss or getting in shape. Really, all we have to do is take small, daily steps toward a healthy approach to eating, exercising, and loving ourselves. There are lots of us who want to be loved, but in reality, it has to start with loving ourselves.

I know this, as I have been exercising for thirty years and have tried all types of pre-contest nutrition plans and have hired the best personal trainers to prepare me to win every contest. Even though I won every contest toward the end of my fitness career, I always had the same feeling after each success: I was not happy with me.

I had forgotten how to love myself, because my mother had frowned at me or shushed me when I said that I loved myself. She thought I was being arrogant or selfish and that it was rude of me to share my success when I won my competitions. In reality, she should have been pleased. She should have celebrated the hard work that I had put into my preparations for all twenty-five contests.

Now, at age fifty, I realize that I do not need her approval or anyone else's. I just need to accept myself as the woman I have become: a strong, driven woman who looks for the good in people, because everyone on this earth has much to offer, and we can all learn from each other. I have done everything that I believed would improve myself, whether it meant having a healthy lifestyle, surrounding myself with amazing, gifted, positive people, learning something about myself every week, or listening to others who needed my guidance.

How many times have we listened to negative people or people who think that their opinion has more value than yours? Really, if we would just look within and love ourselves, the negative self-talk and bullying would go away. We need to reclaim our own inner power, to speak to our souls, to say *thank you* for everything, to say *I love you*. I find that meditation, letting go of stuff, and moving forward every day in a positive way—and doing things like eating well and exercising the way you want to—fill your heart, rejuvenate your soul, and give you permission to pursue with passion the *you* that you have always known was within you. It will be the answer to your prayers.

What are you going to do for yourself today and every day? This is your life. Maybe it is time for you to book a trip to Sedona, Arizona, for an amazing healing retreat. It is your time. Just do it. You are going to thank yourself one day.

I send you much love.

Chapter Nineteen

The Next Fifty Years of My Life

I HAVE BEEN TOLD THAT we learn from the first fifty years of our lives so we can tweak our next fifty years of life. We learn to be more aware of what we want and what we don't want in our lives, and I certainly won't repeat the life lessons I experienced when I had no clue as to what I was doing. I have looked back at the good, the bad, and the oh-my-God moments and have realized that I needed to learn something from everything that happened to me. No, I'm not suggesting that getting raped or being abused by family members or an ex-husband is the ideal way to learn about life. But I have learned that in life we are all here to learn, to embrace life, and to become teachers for others so that we can help them pick up the pieces and rebuild their lives, bodies, and souls.

It does take time to gather the life-pieces of your human soul, to take positive measures, and to make yourself accountable for what happens to you personally. Just take a moment and reflect upon the reasons you've had to experience all those darn challenges, which, at the time, just crept up and hit you like a whirlwind.

When those things happen to me, they usually happen in threes. The first time, I brush it off. The second time, it's very much like the first time but in a different location or event. The third time, I respond, "Okay, I got it. Sheesh." That is usually a message for me to stop what I'm doing, to proceed in a different way, to learn from the situation, and to not repeat it again. Basically, I am making myself more aware of my situations. It does not happen to me very often, but when it does, I totally acknowledge it and stop putting on the brakes, as positive challenges are presenting themselves.

Here is an example of a set of "three" that happened to me last week. One day I got up, and as I was walking toward the washroom, I bent down to pick up something off the floor. As I was coming up, I banged my head on the edge of the wall. No, I did not get hurt, but I did feel it. Then I went downstairs to get a sweater from the front closet, and as I opened the closet door, one of my winter gloves came down and hit the side of my head. At that point, I knew the angels were trying to tell me something, but of course, being the stubborn French woman that I am, I did not really zero in on what the message was.

I had been invited to attend an event that evening to support a friend of mine who was going to be a speaker. As I was sitting at the table with other guests and speakers, a woman behind me lifted her chair and just so slightly brushed my head with her chair. I finally acknowledged that the angels were telling me something, and I said, "Okay, I am ready to listen and find out what your message is." (The lady did apologize, in case some of you were wondering.)

As I sat and listened, I suddenly understood the message from the angels. Part of the message was, "You don't need to be perfect at the start, but with time and practice—and by surrounding yourself with credible men and women—you will be on your way. One day soon, you are going to be busy traveling as an event speaker to share your story and your life's mission." At that moment, I thanked my angels and knew deep within myself that I was going to make a difference, inspiring men and women with my story and guiding them to take a step for the better.

You too can one day experience that kind of message as well.

Yes, I have been through a lot in my life, but I always knew, deep in my soul, that there was light at the end of the tunnel. At times I can be very impatient with life, and I want all the good things to happen immediately. But once I settle down and just focus on what matters, somehow it all works out in the end. With life being so instantaneous, we forget that we need to live for today, not tomorrow or next week.

With that, we must also plan for tomorrow and beyond. Sometimes I get so caught up with personal goals that I live for what's going to take place in six weeks or six months. I tend to forget that I need to live for today, set monthly goals to keep myself grounded, and take it one day at a time.

Please understand that for the past two years I have been working on myself by taking it one day at a time—keeping fit, eating clean, and working toward achieving my personal and business goals on a daily and weekly basis. As a professional athlete, I competed in twenty-five contests, so I was conditioned to set twelve-week goals that included weekly training routines, workouts at the gym six days a week, and six clean meals a day, seven days a week.

When I retired, I had to shift my thinking and not be so hard on myself. Now my workouts are only three to four days a week, and I eat four to five meals a day, five days a week. And I finally enjoy my weekends without feeling guilty. I am so grateful for all the knowledge I gained from the fitness industry. I had so much fun with it.

Now, being fifty, I have learned to be more selective about the people I surround myself with. I value people for who they are and for their personal successes and achievements. But there are times when I enjoy being on my own, working on my next project, or just being with myself. I am enjoying every transition in my life. Sometimes when I receive a phone call or I'm at an appointment, something suddenly comes up that could throw my day off. When that happens, I sit and reflect on what just happened and the potential reason for it, as I just don't know what life experiences are about to present themselves. I don't walk around the house being miserable or feeling sorry for myself, as I know there is always a solution. I deal with those kinds of days by meditating and listening to peaceful, spiritual music, so I can reflect on what lesson I've learned from it and understand how to handle it. We tend to complicate our lives for no reason. Life is very simple, but only you can simplify it for yourself.

My passion is to help women and men, if they are ready to take charge of their own lives. I talk a lot about taking your power back. What I mean by this is that we are here to learn from this life. We are all born with a mission in life, but as we grow up, people we meet or live with have a tendency to tell us their opinions of how our lives should be, and we give up our power to them. Don't you think it is time for you to step up and say to yourself, "I am taking back my personal inner power and doing what I have always wanted to do with my life mission"?

It does take time to heal and to take charge of our lives, but with persistence and the will to take control of ourselves, taking one day at time and surrounding ourselves with quality men and women, our lives will turn around for the better. You need to do it. I always say, "Actions speak louder than words." I am here for you, if you are ready and willing to walk on the path with me.

I know there are days when you wake up in the morning and just feel empty. I've been there, wondering if life can be any better than it is now. The only way you can change your outlook is to think in a positive, grateful way each morning and say thank you to the angels and to God for a peaceful sleep and for keeping you safe. Tell them you are ready to heal and to learn from them how to better your life. Believe that greatness will present itself to you in a very positive way.

Working on yourself takes time, and you need to take the steps that are best for you, not what others think you need to do. You need to do it and feel it and then see the results of taking steps to better yourself. Spend time in daily affirmations, daily life reflections, and gratitude for the person you are at this moment. Keep going forward, and don't look back. You learn from the past what *not* to do or bring or repeat in your life.

You need to focus on the life legacy you want and have always believed that you can have. Everything you have always envisioned for your life, that which you truly deserve, is actually only an arm's length away. You just need to see it and realize that it has always been there for you. You were just unaware of it.

I am so grateful to have beautiful, strong, intelligent daughters, and I have paved the way for them so that they too can reach to the sky for opportunities and greatness. The sky is the limit in all aspects of life—financial, spiritual, emotional, and physical. Every one of my daughters is a piece of me, and I hope that they have learned the morals, ethics, and values of life that I have taught them. I hope they teach their own families as well.

I have known for years that life is very beautiful, even with all the personal challenges that presented themselves to me. I always believed that there was a way to heal. You can take charge of your life and acknowledge your will to live and to make a difference.

I am looking forward to meeting, mentoring, coaching, and inspiring those who are searching for someone like me. I am here for you, and I am so grateful that you are going to let me help you heal, reclaim your life, and celebrate the person that you are: an amazing, beautiful, valuable person, inside and out.

I love people. I love me. I love life. I love my dearest friends and the new friends I haven't met yet. I love my angels, my guides, and the Lord Jesus, as they have never given up on me. I have always known that they were within me and around me. They kept showing me that there was light at the end of the tunnel, that there was great abundance in all of life.

Here's to another fifty years of life lessons for me and the creation of a legacy for you—to keep growing, healing, and valuing yourself.

I love you, and I am grateful.

Je t'aime,
Angelique

CPSIA information can be obtained at www.ICGtesting.com
Printed in the USA
LVOW082331030613

336733LV00001B/36/P